theCONTENT CONNECTION

How to Integrate Thinking and Writing in the Content Areas

CONNECTION

Hilarie N. Staton

Illustrated by Dave Garbot

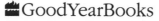
GoodYearBooks

An Imprint of ScottForesman
A Division of HarperCollins*Publishers*

Acknowledgments

The author would like to thank the following people for their help, advice and support:

Sue Abramsky • Judy Wendell • Jo Ann Traub
Jessica Cooper • Judy Iapoce • Patricia George
Kenneth Bierly • Anita Meinbach • Dave Garbot

and, most of all, Joe

Good Year Books
are available for preschool through grade 6 for
every basic curriculum subject plus many enrichment
areas. For more Good Year Books, contact your local
bookseller or educational dealer. For a complete
catalog with information about other Good Year Books,
please write:

Good Year Books
Scott, Foresman and Company
1900 East Lake Avenue
Glenview, IL 60025

ISBN 0-673-46083-5

6   7   8   9   10 – VPI – 99   98   97   96

The CONTENT

How to Integrate Thinking and Writing in the Content Areas

CONNECTION

Contents

Contents

Understanding the
Thinking-Writing-Content Connection
Identifying Thinking Skills

Thinking is how we try to make sense of anything and everything. We take in data through our senses; then we try to create meaning out of the bits and pieces. We organize and process them. We look for patterns, connections, and relationships, and then we make decisions based on our findings. We answer questions like: What's next? Do we like or dislike something and why? How can we use this information to create something new?

Researchers have tried to learn what makes up the process of thinking. They have reached different conclusions, but all agree that it is a complex process made up of many specific skills. Researchers haven't agreed on the names, numbers, or definitions of these skills, only that they exist. We know that literal thinking (the taking in of data) is the basis for the higher-level thinking skills. Benjamin Bloom lists the cognitive skills as knowledge, comprehension, application, analysis, synthesis, and evaluation. In order to perform the skills at the higher end of the list, like synthesis, we must have already performed the skills of knowledge and comprehension.

Jean Piaget discussed how a child's thinking develops. His "Concrete Operations" stage lasts from about ages 7 to 11. These are the students who still need concrete examples, but they are beginning to see new points of view and are developing social awareness. He warns that the individual differences in this group are great, something we must keep in mind when judging students' writing. Some students, he says, may pass into the next stage and will no longer need concrete examples to make connections, see relationships, and do the higher levels of thinking. Our task as teachers is to help students along this path.

The research is interesting, but what really matters to us as teachers is how that research can be used in our classrooms. We know that: students should have the chance to use as many of the thinking skills as possible; we need to give them concrete examples as we introduce new ways of viewing, organizing, and integrating information; and we need to guide them as they stretch their thinking.

Higher-level thinking skills need to be part of a student's daily routine. Some programs introduce thinking skills as a separate activity, apart from content lessons. But students need experience in using the thinking skills where they belong, where they are required for success—in the content areas. They need to see how thinking skills work by watching and evaluating adults as they model their thinking processes. Higher-level questions need to be part of class discussions in science, social studies, and math and students need to think about literature in more abstract ways. They also need to use thinking skills to plan and organize their writing. It's not always easy to emphasize these skills when you're racing the recess bell or force-feeding facts for a state end-of-year test.

1

In order to accomplish this integration, we as teachers must do some serious thinking of our own. We need to develop the skill of asking higher-level questions. We need to remember to ask students to make assumptions and judgments, to use figurative language and comparisons, to apply facts to new situations, and to make generalizations. Students need to think critically about what an author says and about how they can get their own points across.

Students need to practice these thinking skills throughout their schooling, starting in the primary grades. We must encourage them to use these skills in new situations, even where there is no one to guide them. In other words, they must transfer thinking skills from the classroom to daily life. Only when this happens are we truly successful.

But thinking isn't all skills, it's also something almost mystical and magical. It's also a creative, intuitive, inexplicable type of thinking that can't be taught and we must be careful not to crush or overpower it with skills and organization and objectives. This, too, is an important part of the thinking-writing connection.

Linking Thinking and Writing

Thinking involves processing language, both the seen (reading) and the heard (listening). Humans communicate their thinking using language. They can use sign language, spoken language, or written language. Students need to understand that human communication involves all language processes (reading, speaking, listening, and writing). They need many structured experiences in all these language processes. We need to teach, and have students practice, the complex skills and strategies that make up each process, not in isolation, but as part of communicating information.

For example, one of the best ways to foster good writing is to surround the process with talk. Discuss the content, the writing process, students' goals and progress, and the written product itself. Then, after the writing process has been completed, have students share their work. The communication process of writing uses both reading and speaking. By combining these processes, students begin to see how we use writing to communicate our ideas to an audience.

But students often try to out-guess the teacher rather than communicate their thinking. They fear being wrong, so they only write what they believe the teacher wants to hear. We teachers are at fault, too, because we often require only the very basic types of writing (such as fill-in-the-blanks and short answers).

Writing works with thinking in another way. The act of writing often helps us clarify the subject about which we are writing. Studies have shown that writing can increase the amount of thinking that is taking place. As we manipulate the raw data, we see new connections, find better reasons, and find new motives. In other words we discover meaning. As our thinking becomes clearer, so does our writing. Students who write about content understand it better and remember it longer. Haven't you had the experience of trying to explain something when suddenly everything becomes clear? That missing connection is suddenly made. You understand it better and are able to express yourself more clearly. We must make students aware of writing as a way to clarify their ideas and to communicate their ideas to others.

No matter what type of writing we're doing, we begin with literal thinking. Then we organize, analyze, and make decisions about these observations, perceptions, and research data. We evaluate our information. Do we need more data? How do the individual items relate to one another? How do they relate to the topic? How do they apply to the writer? As we manipulate the data, we use higher-level thinking skills to analyze, evaluate, and synthesize. We also use them as we revise. That's when we evaluate and rethink what we've written. We look at its organization, validity, intelligibility, and purpose. Thinking skills, both lower and higher skills, are an inherent part of the writing process. We just need to be sure students are using many different higher-level thinking skills and that they are comfortable with them.

Both informal writing (such as journals) and formal writing (such as reports and essays) use a variety of thinking skills. In informal writing, journals can be a workplace for the thinking process. Brainstorming, organizing, discerning relationships, and drawing conclusions can all take place. Each type of formal writing uses a different set of thinking skills. A "compare and contrast" paragraph will use different thinking skills than a haiku poem. Teachers need to be aware of the thinking skills required for each type of writing and assign a variety of types.

We must model the thinking skills and give students practice in using them. If we assign an editorial without teaching the thinking skills (such as finding and selecting pertinent facts), then we must be prepared to accept simple, unsupported, and disorganized writing. "Because" becomes an acceptable reason unless students have been taught how to determine which details support their position. Only after they practice and understand these skills can we expect them to use the skills competently in graded writing assignments.

Writing can not serve its major purpose, to communicate meaning, unless the writer has used many thinking skills to observe, organize, support, create, manipulate, analyze, and evaluate. Writing is a thinking process. Good writing depends on good thinking, and thinking becomes better with writing.

Thinking and Writing in the Content Areas

What is it we need to do to help students become effective thinkers and writers? Studies show that the more a person writes, the more comfortable that person is with writing, the better their writing becomes, and the more they think about the content, the more their memory of the content improves. Therefore, first we must be sure that we allow students time to think and to write about subjects they feel are important. And we must ask them to write not only sentences and answers to our questions, but longer, more purposeful assignments—writing that communicates meaning to a specific audience.

In order to make the writing meaningful, we must integrate writing assignments into all parts of the curriculum. The writing, both informal and formal, should come from the topics discussed in literature, social studies, science, health, and other content areas. Thinking and writing skills should be taught as they relate to what is being studied, *not* in an isolated "English" exercise.

First, students must understand that writing is communication and use it as such, time and time again. They can use it to teach their peers or to entertain younger students. They can re-enact a historical event or provide an account of their scientific experiments. They need to communicate in writing and see a response from an audience.

Second, we must teach students the writing process and allow them time to explore each step. They must become so involved in writing and so familiar with the writing process that it becomes second nature to them. The only way this can happen is if we demand they use it whenever they do formal writing — in any class.

Third, we need to create an environment in which students are excited about writing and feel comfortable doing it. We must encourage inexperienced writers and give them chances to write without fear, whether it be in personal journals, learning logs, or class assignments. A combination of teacher-assigned topics and student-generated topics can foster growth in writing skills and content knowledge while motivating students. Teacher-assigned topics can provide practice in specific forms, thinking and writing skills, and content. When students take part in creating their own assignments, they develop more confidence and their fluency increases.

Fourth, we must provide students with instructional support, encouragement, and guidance whenever they write. If we do this during the writing process, rather than as corrections on a final copy, students will better understand the process, thinking skills, and the mechanics involved in writing. Their work will be of a higher quality. Students must learn to be supportive, too, so that they become a resource and guide for each other. Students who know they will get help along the way are not afraid to take chances, to stretch, to communicate, and to write. For writing to flourish, students and teachers must respect each others' ideas, suggestions, and creativity.

Last, our evaluation must change its focus from how well students master writing mechanics to how well they communicate appropriate meaning. The mechanics are not forgotten, just put in their proper place, at the end of the writing process. We set standards for students in both communications and mechanics; and we continually raise them, so students continue to grow. And we must be willing to accept the creative, unusual and daring.

When a person understands what is expected of him or her, has the necessary thinking and writing skills, and feels comfortable writing, writing becomes something special. Suddenly, that person is able to write in new and interesting ways. Suddenly, people understand what that person is trying to say. Suddenly, he or she is a "real" writer.

Teaching the Writing Process
Planning for Teaching

Teachers begin thinking about a writing assignment long before the students are aware of it. We must decide what the objectives of the assignment will be and whether content or form will be stressed. When there are clear objectives for the assignment, they become the basis for revising, editing, and the final evaluation.

As we think about the objectives, we must balance the different parts of the assignment. If you are emphasizing the analysis of complex social studies content, then require a writing form that is familiar to students, such as a personal letter. If you are requiring a complex writing form, such as a comparison essay, use familiar or highly motivating content.

We must decide what skills, both thinking and writing skills, the student will need and whether or not we'll have to teach and/or model them. If we want students to use clustering, we must give them practice in clustering before it is required as part of the process. If the information is to come from books, we must model how to find it and give students experience in note-taking. If the information is to come from a movie, students must be taught the necessary listening skills.

Each type of writing demands a different set of thinking skills, so we must be sure students have the skills they need before they begin the assignment. They need to know sequencing for a recipe, observation for a friendly letter, and imagery for a poem. Students need to understand the use of pre-writing organizers, so they can organize their information easily. If they are to compare how a holiday is celebrated in two different cultures, they need to know how to structure a "compare and contrast" article. Students need training and prompting to evaluate, synthesize, and apply facts in their writing. Certainly, they do not need to be skillful in everything, but they do need to be familiar with the writing process and with the necessary thinking skills before they begin independent assignments. The better prepared they are in the skills necessary to the writing assignment, the easier it will be for them.

In order for students to practice the writing process, it should be part of all content classes. It can be done as a class, small group or individual assignment, or different combinations can be created. For instance, a small group can research and organize the information and then each member can do his or her own writing. Or an individual can do research and then share his or her information with the group, which creates a piece of "group" writing. Small groups might create a cluster about a math process they've just learned. As the class discusses and edits the cluster, they become familiar with the math process. Individuals can use this knowledge to write a description of the process. These combinations emphasize practice in the whole writing process without having students do it on their own.

Motivating Students to Write

Besides teaching the necessary skills, we should never forget to excite and motivate students. Just having skills and knowing the process doesn't cause the spark that creates outstanding writers. It's the excitement of the content and of the process that creates excitement in the writing. We have to plan to make that excitement happen. In order to give students confidence and to create this interest, we should surround the writing process with talk. As a class, brainstorm all the possible, probable, creative and even silly ideas related to the topic. Discuss it, share it, interpret it in different ways, interest the students. In class, in small groups and in informal conferences, have students talk about the content, the writing process, and their problems and successes.

You can also spark motivation by involving students in the planning process. Students have a greater sense of ownership when they make their own decisions about their topic, audience, genre, and methods. If your goal is to involve students in the subject matter, give them the chance to choose their topics and forms. Let them peruse a large selection of content resources before they decide on their topic. Other times, assign specific topics, audiences, or forms so students have a chance to explore all types of writing.

Modeling the Writing Process

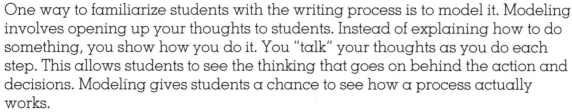

One way to familiarize students with the writing process is to model it. Modeling involves opening up your thoughts to students. Instead of explaining how to do something, you show how you do it. You "talk" your thoughts as you do each step. This allows students to see the thinking that goes on behind the action and decisions. Modeling gives students a chance to see how a process actually works.

The Language Experience Approach is a very valuable way to model writing for students of all grades. In college, I was taught that Language Experience was a reading approach to use with non-readers. I've since learned it can be much more. In Language Experience, something is used as the stimuli, maybe a field trip or a science experiment. The class writes together with the students dictating sentences and the teacher writing down their suggestions. The theory is that since the words and ideas are theirs, they will be able to read it, and they usually can.

In retrospect, though, I realize I used this approach in the wrong way. I didn't follow the writing process. I wrote down what they said and left it uncorrected or automatically corrected as I wrote. My first copy was clean. I didn't edit or change much. I spelled everything correctly and the chart was neat enough to be posted immediately after the writing. I lied to my students about how the writing process really works. Because of my model, they thought their first draft should be a clean, correct, and completed document. I didn't show them the real way I write: the misspellings, changed words, moved paragraphs, and grammar corrections. They thought that planning, revising, and editing were punishment for not have a perfect first draft.

If we model the actual writing process, students will learn how and when to gather, organize, and write facts and ideas. They will learn to pour forth ideas and then evaluate how they fit together. They will learn to reorganize, add, or subtract material and finally to correct mechanical mistakes. If students follow this process during all writing assignments and in every class, they will see that the process is the same no matter what the content.

At first this modeling should go through all the steps in the writing process to give students a chance to see how the "whole" works. Later, you can follow one or two steps with the class (in any subject area) to deepen their understanding of each individual step. They can perform the rest of the steps as independent assignments, in small groups, or not at all. For instance, have students cluster or categorize all the types of animals they know during a science lesson, or ask the class as a whole to revise a social studies paper written by a previous class. As students become comfortable with the steps, give them more freedom.

One way to help students produce coherent writing is to have them do the work in class. Take time during the content class to write about the content. After all, while they are writing they are thinking and learning about the content's facts and ideas. During this time, you can model skills, teach how the parts of the content relate to each other, and hold mini-conferences. You can use these conferences to guide students, keep track of their progress, and reteach skills. Students can't leave everything until the last moment; they can't skip a step; and they can't remain stuck for long. They can get help in selecting an organizer or finding a better way to convey their meaning. You can teach them exactly what they need to know and they can put it into immediate use.

Using the writing process in content lessons takes planning, but most of it is done during the "thinking" that you, the teacher, do beforehand. Once you've chosen objectives, content, and resources, you're able to spend your time as a teacher, guiding your students to become good writers.

Informal Writing
▼

Informal writing is free writing done without the threat of correction. It is thinking in written form. Journals, logs, and writing loops are forms of informal writing. They encourage the writer to write down his or her thoughts quickly without correction. Sometimes these are about a specific topic (focused free writing); other times students write informally about anything that comes to mind. As this is done, relationships, connections, and questions that need to be answered become clearer. Some forms, like learning logs, are meant to help students clarify their thinking about specific content topics. In any of these types of writing, you can see the thinking going on. You read students' observations, see how they came to them, and determine if they've identified the crucial relationships, values, and generalizations. You can guide their thinking through the questions you ask in a written dialogue or through focused free writing activities. This writing can help you and the students determine the next step, be it in a personal relationship or a science unit.

Because we have not required much writing from students, many are hesitant to write. They write a few sentences and then they are sure they're done. Since they haven't had much practice, they are fearful of writing longer pieces, so they don't do it very well. In order for them to feel more comfortable with writing, they need to write and to write more at one sitting. Not all of this writing need be graded. Personal journals and learning logs are good ways to get them writing. Then, when a longer, more structured writing assignment comes along, they are no longer afraid to spend the necessary time in the writing stage.

Informal Personal Writing

Teachers are always looking for new ways to encourage students to write more and for a longer period of time. One way to do so is with informal personal writing. These personal types of writing can inspire non-writing students to write because they enjoy the topic—usually themselves. The goal of informal writing is to write, not to have a finished, polished product. By the way, when you assign something like this, it is a good idea to provide a model. Do it yourself. Let students see you, the teacher, as a writer.

Peter Elbow suggests many forms of informal writing. In some writing is sustained for a period of time without stopping, organizing, or correcting. No subject restrictions are made, only that the writer keep writing. Students soon find their writing heads toward one topic, and they begin to write all they know about it. These topics might concern events or topics from their studies. As students realize they have something to say, they become more confident and their writing improves.

Personal journals also encourage sustained writing. In these journals, students write each day about whatever they want. Expect everything from boy-watching to baseball and movies. These private diary-type journals are read and answered (but not corrected) by the teacher. Students not only begin to enjoy writing, but soon they write more and more. They realize that writing is communicating and that they must write clearly for the reader to understand what they are trying to say

Personal journals are meant to be a private communication. It takes time for a relationship to develop between the writer and the responder, but in a trusting atmosphere students will feel free to speak their "thinking." Teachers can guide students to higher levels of thinking by the questions they ask—no matter what the topic. This writing should be shared with a larger audience only when the writer agrees..

A warning about personal journals: they have some inherent problems that teachers should understand before assigning them. Many teachers comment how quickly their students open up in this type of journal. This means touchy issues like child abuse, substance abuse, or illegal activities might be part of a journal entry. Be sure you know what you will do if a student begins writing about such subjects. Consider sharing your stand with students at the beginning so no one feels betrayed. Will you break this confidence to get the student help? If so, how will you explain this breaking of trust to the student? We have to address these kinds of issues when people share their inner lives with us.

Many types of thinking appear in personal journals. Teachers can use pertinent questions in their dialogue to guide students to higher levels of thinking. For example, here is a sample from the personal journal of a sixth-grade student. Notice how the teacher's responses guide the student away from emotional responses into problem solving.

Student's Journal Entry: I was in a fight with a friend. We were on the playground and there is this jungle gym. I had never climbed to the top of the jungle gym before and this was my first time. I was frightened. My friend came over and started shaking the bars so I fell. A teacher came over and said, "Go to the nurse's office, and next time don't do something if your afraid."

Teacher (in written response to journal entry): Are you all right, Jessica? What do you think about what happened to you? Are you sorry you tried something new?

Student: Yes I'm alright. I thought that the teacher yelled at me for something that I couldn't have stopped. I wanted to climb to the top of the jungle gym and when I was at the top I felt proud. That teacher had no idea about who's fault the accident was.

Teacher: What would you have done if you were the teacher?

Student: I would have gotten the story from both girls and decided who started the trouble and what they should have to do as a punishment.

Teacher: I know when I'm on playground duty I'm always afraid that someone will get hurt. Do you think safety is so important that we should limit the use of the equipment?

Student: No. But I think the kids should know the rules of the playground so accidents won't happen as often. Just because one kid hurts another all the kids shouldn't have to suffer. The one who should suffer is the kid who started trouble.

Teacher: I agree with your ideas. Now, how can we make sure they know the rules? Can you suggest a way teachers can be more fair?

Student: We can have an assembly on rules for the playground or even have a set of rules posted out by the playground. Teachers should not just accuse one child or another. They should know what happened and then make a fair judgment.

The teacher guided the student away from her emotional response into problem solving. The teacher might follow up on the student's suggestions by helping refine the assembly idea into one that can be presented to the principal. The teacher has led the student into thinking of broader issues, how they can be solved and how to refine thoughts on an issue. This guidance of the thinking process is possible because of the open communication that has developed between the two people.

Also in this sample, the teacher has modeled mechanics and grammar. The student's use of these may not show an immediate result, but over several months, they will improve.

Personal writing is a less structured form of writing. It can help students appreciate writing as communication and can get them to do more sustained writing. But nothing comes cheaply. It takes time—some each day—and the results may be slow in coming.

Learning Logs
▼

Learning logs and academic journals are more structured and more focused than personal journals, but they still leave room for individual differences and creativity. In her book *Coming to Know*, Nancy Atwell defines learning logs:

> Logs are spiral-bound notebooks to last a whole school year, one for each subject area. Children's log entries are informal, tentative, first draft, and brief, usually consisting of no more than ten minutes of focused free writing. The teacher poses questions and situations or sets themes that invite students to observe, speculate, list, chart, web, brainstorm, role-play, ask questions, activate prior knowledge, collaborate, correspond, summarize, predict, or shift to a new perspective: in short, to participate in their own learning.*

Logs like these are a chance for students to use writing to clarify their thinking or to take their thinking a step further. Because of this, the students are required to write something, but their entries are not graded or corrected. Their entries are considered part of the thinking-learning process. The goal is to get students to use the writing process to improve their thinking and it is amazing how many different types of thinking can be found in a very simple learning log. The teacher can read and comment on learning logs periodically rather than keeping a dialogue going with students.

Learning logs aren't necessarily done every day or in every subject, but they are used often to help students feel comfortable with writing as part of the thinking process. Some entries might even create enough interest that students use them as the basis for a structured writing assignment.

*Atwell, Nancie, ed. *Coming to Know, Writing to Learn in the Intermediate Grades.* Portsmouth, NH: Heinemann, 1990, p. xvii.

The focus questions or themes that teachers ask students to write about in their learning logs can be similar to test questions, more structured writing assignments, or discussion questions. The questions should focus students' attention on the important content, thinking skills, and relationships. Students can write about how they feel about a subject, such as slavery, or how it would feel to be a slave. They can write all they know about a topic such as butterflies, or they can draw an organizer of a butterfly's life cycle. They can predict what will happen next in a story (or in history) or create their own ending. This is a good time to practice higher-level thinking skills, because students won't feel threatened by a final product. Ask questions that require students to reach conclusions, predict, evaluate figurative language, make comparisons, personalize information, or make generalizations. Students can apply information to new situations or can relate new facts to their prior knowledge. The possibilities are endless.

Learning logs can be used in any class, in a variety of ways. Students might brainstorm and write in their science log all the weather words and phrases they know. A class list can be compiled and students can then, in journals or together, categorize these words. New, technical words can be introduced and fit into the categories. Another day, students might use their logs to observe the weather or predict how they would feel if they were caught in a certain type of weather.

In social studies, students can use their logs to relate past information to future lessons. For instance, after a lesson on the geography of the Plains states, students might be asked to predict what the first settlers would see and how those settlers (who were used to forests and mountains) would feel after a few months on the Plains. After they share their predictions, individuals or groups can write questions to be answered during their study of the early pioneers, or they can create a play or posters advertising the Plains or any of 101 other presentations.

In math, students can describe the steps they take to complete a process or to solve a word problem. Small groups can share and refine their steps into classroom charts. In health class, students might write about how they would feel after an unusual occurrence, such as a sleepless night or strenuous exercise. In physical education logs students can record and evaluate their performances in different sports or describe how a certain activity is done.

A literature journal is a learning log about the books and stories students are reading. It is often a cross between a learning log and a personal journal and is sometimes called a "literature response journal." In it, students do focused free writing in which they discuss their feelings toward a book, topic, or characters. They might answer questions like: Would you like to meet the main character and what would you talk about? Do you think the author did a good job of describing the setting? Would you like to visit this place? Why or why not? In a dialogue journal, the teacher can suggest new ways of thinking about a book or story while the student is still reading it.

Here is an example of a literature journal:

Student's Journal Entry: I just started Super Fudge. It's a funny book. I like Fudge the best.

Teacher (in a written response to the entry): I like *Superfudge*, too. I thought Peter and Fudge acted pretty strangely when they learned their mother was going to have a baby. Why do you think they did that?

Student: I don't think Fudge and Peter like one another. They always fight. Maybe they don't want someone else to fight with.

Teacher: Have you come to the part where Fudge acts like a baby? Why do you think he did that?

Student: Yes. He's mad that another person is around. He's want attention like the baby. He is jealous.

Teacher: Do you think the boys will ever get used to the baby?

Student: No. They don't have many friends so they'll be stuck with one another all day long. It's going to be a *long* summer.

Teacher: How do you think the baby might change what they do during their summer days? I sure wouldn't want to be in the middle of their fights!

Student: Well they might have to take care of the baby or babysit. They won't be able to listen to tapes real loud or the television real loud if the baby's sleeping.

After writing in learning logs, students can share their thinking in pairs, small groups, or in whole-class settings. This sharing not only broadens their information base and helps correct inaccuracies, but it develops a tolerance for different points of view and ways of thinking. When students read or discuss their entries a teacher can identify the types of thinking going on, gaps in prior knowledge, and how well the students are assimilating the information. Then they can adapt lessons to strengthen limited prior knowledge or to correct faulty thinking skills.

Other types of journals include response or reaction journals and observation journals. In a reaction journal the writer responds or reacts to something specific. It can be anything from an experiment to a novel to a person. Student responses can be guided by questions from the teacher or their entries can be general reactions. An observation journal records the writer's observations of one subject over a period of time. For instance, as part of a science unit on plants, students might record their day-by-day observations of a seed they've planted.

Learning logs can be used in any subject to help both the student and teacher understand the content and the thinking processes. The goals for any journal writing are the same: to encourage writing, to broaden thinking skills, to communicate with another human being, and, sometimes, to give the teacher a glimpse into the head of a child.

The Structured Writing Process

Informal writing often has no required structure and sometimes no required topic. The work is unpublished and sometimes not even finished. With formal writing, we have different goals. We usually work toward a finished, polished, published product for a specific audience. The audience may be a business, a whole class, the general public, our parents, and, of course, the teacher. Our purpose might be: to order something, to create an imaginary world to entertain people, to convince someone to change their mind about a topic; or to inform people about important events. We often have to take a stand, use a point of view or examine an issue. We use text structures to help us get our meaning across. Above all, structured writing is communication. Therefore, the meaning of the writing is of paramount importance, something which we must constantly remind students. This is also true of informal writing, but because structured writing has more formal purposes and audiences, it has to be better thought out, organized, and presented. In order to do this, writers use a series of steps called "the writing process."

The writing process contains the following steps: pre-writing, writing, revising, editing, and publishing the finished copy. The pre-writing step includes: understanding the assignment; thinking about and researching the topic; and organizing the information. The writing step involves writing a first draft. The revision and editing steps include: rereading; rethinking; holding conferences about meaning; rewriting for better meaning; and evaluating for mechanical mistakes. The final step, the finished copy, involves producing and presenting the final copy in any one of a hundred ways. Students need to understand that the writing step is only one part of the process and the other steps are equally important to good writing.

Each step and each activity uses different thinking skills. For instance, pre-writing organizational activities use thinking skills like identifying cause and effect, sequence, and identifying supporting details, while the revising and editing stage uses evaluation skills, like making judgments.

The writing process, as a whole, must be modeled and discussed for students to understand it. The amount of time spent on each step will depend on the type of assignment, the students, and the goals of the teacher. If the assignment draws mainly on prior knowledge (maybe recent lessons about plants) students will need less time for the pre-writing step. Early in the year, you will need to plan more time for conferences. If students are to "publish" their writing, for instance in a book that will be located in the library, they will need more time to create the final product.

Different people take a different amount of time to complete each step and so travel through the process at different rates. At any one time, expect students to be in many different stages of a writing assignment. Some will find one step harder than the others. Some will spend more time organizing while others spend it revising. The progress of assignments, especially long-term ones like reports, should be monitored closely. When necessary, students should be prompted to go on to the next step or slowed down so each step is given enough attention.

The writing process is not necessarily a linear one. We often move back and forth between steps. Personally, I take a lot of time in the preparation and revising steps and less time in the writing and editing steps. However, while writing, I often reorganize and I do extra research while revising. Other writers take less time in the pre-writing phase and more in the writing. If students are limited to a specific amount of time and sequence, some will end up bored and some with their work unfinished. The "magic" and flexibility of writing will disappear.

From the beginning phase, pre-writing, to the sharing of a completed work, students should feel that they are creating something. The writing process is to make life easier for a writer, not to force him or her into a mold or to go through a series of steps. However, the beginning step, the pre-writing phase, is where most students are insecure. If we can ease them through that successfully, we can get them through the rest, for they will know where they are going and how to get there.

The Pre-Writing Phase

The first step in the writing process is a crucial one, but it is often slighted. Pre-writing contains three processes: understanding the assignment, gathering data, and organizing the data. Each requires different thinking, reading, and study skills for success.

Some students panic as soon as they read an essay question or hear that they must write a report or story. But when students analyze the assignment, become excited about the topic, and organize their thoughts, the writing becomes less of a threat.

Analyze assignments with students. Model how you tear apart assignments to determine what the final product should be, who it will be for, and what it will cover. Model different types of assignments so students become familiar with the various components, like introductions, conclusions, and comparison paragraphs.

Students need a strong base in understanding the vocabulary of writing assignments. With this understanding, they can better determine the purpose, structure, and content necessary for the writing. Define the writing vocabulary as well as specific content words for each assignment. Teach them what is expected of them when they encounter specific key words.

In the following example, the writing key words are in bold and the content key words are underlined.

> **Pretend** you are a <u>colonist</u> living in <u>Boston</u> in <u>1775</u>. Write a **letter** to **someone in England explaining** to them your **feelings** about <u>Parliament's actions</u> against the American colonies.

For this lesson, we must not only teach a letter's form, but we must also teach what explaining feelings entails. We have to get students to identify (maybe by circling) the key words in directions, so that they don't ignore items critical to a correct answer (for this question the place and year). They need to organize themselves by listening and reacting (as a Boston colonist would) to Parliament's actions, so they don't forget key facts as they become emotional in their letter.

Students must transfer their understanding of the requirements and purposes of each type of writing (such as for a book, friendly letter or comparison essay) from English class to the content area. Students should have strategies to deal with words that reoccur in content writing (such as compare and contrast, and cause and effect). These strategies should help them begin the search for data and organize for writing. On the following list are some common words that are important in understanding writing assignments.

Key Words in Writing Assignments

Question words: describe, discuss, explain, compare, contrast, state, list, trace, problem and solution, cause and effect, opinion, setting, character, theme

Forms: story, letter, essay, diary, speech, editorial, interview, poem, script, article

---

Learning how to approach different types of writing can mean the difference between action and total frustration when students encounter an essay question. In New York State, essay questions appear on the state's sixth-grade test. By teaching students how to deal with key words, we prepare them for the types of writing they will be expected to do during all of their school and working life.

For students who have trouble coping with essays, teach specific text organizers and even phrases to use for each type of question (see page 41). Other students might benefit from the strategy of turning the question into a statement to use as an opening sentence. These strategies ease students' fear of what they have to write, so they can concentrate on the content.

Students must also analyze the assignment to determine their audience. If they are writing a friendly letter to a peer, they will use different language, facts, and ideas than if they are writing for kindergarten students or to a business. Students should be able to integrate their purpose and their audience. What do they want their audience to enjoy, learn, or understand from the writing?

Answering questions like these can help focus their preparation and guide their writing. Once they know what is expected of them, they can proceed independently and with confidence. However, this independence takes time to develop.

After students understand what they will be writing about, they can begin to collect data. They can use information from prior knowledge, books (reference, library, and textbooks), audio-visual sources, and interviews. They can decide what resources are appropriate. You can guide them by limiting their selection, and you should make sure they have experience with as many types of resources as possible. Students should not ignore the information they already possess and should be encouraged to use it as a beginning point for their research.

If students are to do research, as they must for many of the activities in this book, they need experience in taking notes. One way to practice note-taking is by having students read a short selection, and then close the book and write notes about what they just read. As they become more confident, they will be able to reword ideas and not feel that they have to use the source's exact words. This can be done with short listening assignments as well. Organizers can help organize and limit their notes to the pertinent topics.

The activities in this book emphasize various pre-writing strategies that develop thinking skills, such as brainstorming and comparison. These strategies help students prepare for the assignment and force them to think of the data in new ways. Some activities use several pre-writing strategies: one for gathering data and one for organizing it. In some cases, organizers are given, or chosen, before the research is done, so that the data is organized while it is being collected.

These pre-writing techniques and strategies should be taught to students before they need these strategies in an independent writing assignment. They are defined and discussed in the following section. They can be integrated into content lessons: to supplement a lesson, as an evaluation activity, or instead of a complete writing assignment. For example, you can introduce a science lesson by clustering important terms. You can model how to create a cluster and then have the class continue the process, or individuals can do it and then share their clusters with the class. An organizer can show the causes of a historical situation or the steps necessary to solve a math problem. Use a story map to help students understand a story in their reading books. The class can create an organizer and then each student can use it as the basis of his or her writing. As students become familiar with these techniques, they will feel comfortable using them independently to develop their thoughts and ideas for writing.

The following information on pre-writing strategies and techniques is to help you, the teacher, understand them, their purposes, and their possible uses. Also included is an activity sheet to introduce each technique to the students. You might have students keep a folder of the examples. That way they can choose an appropriate technique when one is not specified. This should be only one of many times students use the technique. Remember these strategies and techniques fit in all areas of the curriculum.

Questions

A useful pre-writing strategy is for the writer to ask and/or answer questions about the content, form, and process necessary to do the writing. Content questions can stimulate thinking, analyze ideas, and develop concepts and relationships (What happens when a volcano erupts?) or force them to view things in new ways (Pretend you are the house you live in. What do you think of the people living in you?). Writing questions can help students organize the data for a specific form (What will happened first?) or guide their research (Where can you find information about this person?).

The types of questions asked will determine the thinking skills students use. At first, the questions should follow the thinking process, showing students how to go from lower-level thinking (observation) to higher level thinking (synthesis). For instance, students might answer several questions about two or three mammals (information), then questions comparing their traits (comparison), and finally a question about the traits that are common to all mammals (generalization). They might need this information to write a scientist's journal entry.

As students become proficient, questions can emphasize the higher levels of thinking without the steps that lead up to them. After reading a novel, students might be asked how the main character and setting created the climax (evaluation and synthesis). Advanced students won't need the specific questions about characters, setting, and where they intersect which would lead up to this synthesis. Less advanced students would.

By giving students a list of specific questions to answer before they begin writing, you can control the direction their thinking and writing will take. However, more motivation and excitement is generated when the whole class, small groups, or individuals write the questions they think should be answered in the writing. This involvement will carry over into their writing, making it more personal and giving them a greater stake in creating a final product of which they are proud.

The activity "Purple Mountain's Majesty" (page 105) uses content questions to guide a student's geology research. These questions force students to analyze and evaluate data and to use it in a creative way (personification).

Name _____   **Date** _____

Sometimes writers use questions to plan their work. They ask themselves the questions that they feel should be answered in their writing. Then, they make sure they know the answers before they begin writing. They use those answers in their writing.

Question: Who did it happen to?
Answer: *Wilbur the pig and his owner Zuckerman.*

Question: When did it happen?
Answer: *After Zuckerman talked about killing Wilbur.*

Question: Where did it happen?
Answer: *At the pigpen.*

Question: What happened?
Answer: *The spider web had "some pig" written on it.*

Question: Why did it happen?
Answer: *Because Charlotte wanted to create "a mircle" to save Wilbur.*

Write five questions that should be answered in an article that introduces a new classmate.

1.

2.

3.

4.

5.

One strategy used to plan a story before the writing begins is a story map. Story maps list the important elements of a story, such as characters and setting. These can be in the form of questions, a chart, or a story frame. Story maps are easily adapted by using more sophisticated terminology and elements. A general story map can be used in many situations (Where does the story take place?). You can develop more specific story maps for specific writing assignments. For the activity "Godzilla on Broadway" (page 101) a story map might include the questions: What animal is the story about? Where does it suddenly appear?

Story maps can also be used as a reading and content study strategy. They can guide students to understand a historical event or a scientific experiment or to examine a story they have read. Story maps can also help students determine the pertinent facts for a math word problem, either one they have to solve or one they are creating.

In the activity "All the News!" (page 117) a listing activity helps students choose their topic. Then students answer basic story map questions to develop the details for a newspaper article. Students must have a good grasp of the content and be able to predict how events might happen as they integrate their content knowledge and an imaginary setting, characters, and events.

Name _____   **Date**_____

Writers think and plan their story before they begin writing. A story map helps organize your ideas before you begin writing. It also makes sure you have all the important details. Story maps come in different forms. Sometimes they are a list of questions, other times a chart.

Fill in this story map about a story you'd like to write some day.

Main character	
Other characters	
Where the story takes place	
What happens	
When it happens	
Why it happens	

Brainstorming

Brainstorming is a common pre-writing strategy. During this process, the writer (or the whole class) writes down everything he or she can think of about the topic. Everything—correct, incorrect, and tangential—is acceptable. Unless you are creating a cluster, nothing is organized. The purpose is to stimulate as many thoughts as possible and to create an outpouring of ideas.

Brainstorming is especially effective in large and small groups, because the ideas of one person will stimulate those of another. This allows the list to include many different ideas and gives all students a chance to contribute. It is an excellent way of freeing more structured thinkers and of helping students with limited ideas expand their thinking. Often they learn new ways to make connections and build ideas when they see how their classmates do it.

Brainstorming sessions can be used to develop writing topics, provide details about one topic, or expand the scope of a topic. This strategy fits into any content area and can be added at any point in a lesson.

Most of the activities in this book can be enhanced by group brainstorming before the topics are chosen. Many require individual brainstorming to create lists or clusters during the pre-writing stage.

Brainstorming

Name _____   **Date** _____

Creating a storm in your brain—that's "brainstorming." To brainstorm, list everything you can think of about a topic, even if it sounds silly or doesn't quite fit. One idea leads to another and sometimes a silly one will spark another, not so silly one. Be creative—put down everything you think of.

Here is a brainstorming list about a rock: round, rough, smooth, small, huge, hard, flakes, used to build walls and fences, used as a weapon, used to make stone soup, has fossils in it, used as a door stop, good luck charm, washed by the sea and streams, grey, sparkles, flecks of color, cuts.

Now, choose a person you know. Brainstorm everything you can think of about that person, and write your thoughts here.

Lists

One of the simplest and most common pre-writing strategies is to create a list. Its purpose is to make sure you don't forget anything.

On most lists items can be placed anywhere (List your five favorite activities). Other more structured lists have a specific sequence or order (Pretend you have a lot of errands to do today. List them in the order that you'll do them.). Lists are often done as a first pre-writing step or after brainstorming. Brainstorming, sequencing, and analysis are thinking skills often used in creating lists.

In the activity "Godzilla on Broadway" (page 101) students take notes from non-fiction articles about two diverse subjects. Then they join diverse facts from their notes in creative ways. They use this list as the basis for imaginary events in a story. By creating the list before writing the story, they can play with unusual combinations to trigger story ideas.

Lists

A list is a simple way to keep track of items. Each item is clearly stated in a word or phrase. Lists help us include all the necessary information in our writing.

List of chores:
    clean bedroom
    set dinner table
    vacuum living room

List of friends and from where:
    Jo Ann - at school
    Judy - at Grandma's
    Carole - at camp

Make a list of five people to whom you'd like to give a present. Next to each name, list something you might give them if you had a million dollars.

1.

2.

3.

4.

5.

Clustering* is a form of brainstorming. A cluster includes a central word or phrase, which is circled, and all related thoughts are clustered around that word. When you create a cluster, you organize your thoughts as you add them, but you should not waste time on organizing. It is more important to keep the words and ideas flowing. No two clusters will be the same, none are wrong. Each tells what that person knows, thinks, or feels about the topic. The following is my cluster about clusters:

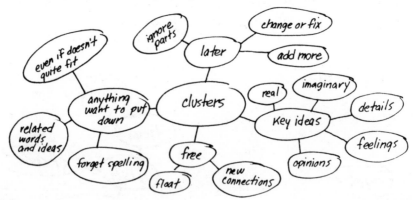

Maps and webs are similar to clusters, but they emphasize the organization more than the brainstorming. A semantic map or semantic web is a more conscious cluster about a specific word. The clustering of words, thoughts and ideas allows us to express all we know about a topic. It is free association, which shows the relationships of ideas. It allows us to play with words and phrases early in the writing process.

Many different thinking processes are used during clustering, especially those from the part of the brain that is often forgotten—the right side. We tap into words and phrases we might not discover otherwise. Since clusters are just words and phrases, they are less threatening to students than writing sentences, essays, or stories. They are more likely to express a wide variety of ideas.

Students should be given many opportunities to use clustering before they use it as an independent pre-writing strategy. This is easy, because clusters fit anywhere. At the beginning of a unit, clustering can help teachers determine students' prior knowledge. Students (and teachers) can plan their research to fill in these gaps. Clusters can help students recall what they've just read, heard, or watched. They can be done with the whole class, by small groups, or as individual activities. Clusters created by the whole class can be used by individuals as the basis for a writing assignment. This experience of writing from a class cluster gives them confidence and a chance to see how many different ways the same information can be used. To expand the information base of students, have them share individual clusters with the class or in small groups. This allows individuals with sparse prior knowledge to add to their store of information. They are able to build stronger images and to write with more confidence. They write more than in the past. They feel they have already done the hard work—the thinking. Now all they have to do is expand the cluster's details into sentences.

The activity "A Wonderful Place" (page 67) asks students to create a cluster around the word "fair." They use their own experiences and those from *Charlotte's Web* or other books to create the cluster. Afterwards, students analyze what they know of a fair to create their own imaginary adventures for a story.

*For further explanation of clustering and exercises for adults, see Gabriele Lusser Rico, *Writing the Natural Way*, St. Martin's Press, 1983.

25

Name _____   **Date**_____

A cluster is one way to brainstorm before you write. To create a cluster, write the key word or phrase in the center circle. Then brainstorm everything you can think of that goes with that key word. Write down all the words and phrases, even if they don't quite fit. Attach each word or phrase to the key word or to one of the other words where it fits. Many words can be attached together. Don't stop, but keep going until you have put down everything you can think of.

Here is a beginning
cluster about
the ocean.

Here is how the
cluster grows.

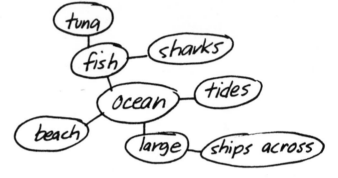

When you finish a cluster it covers many ideas.

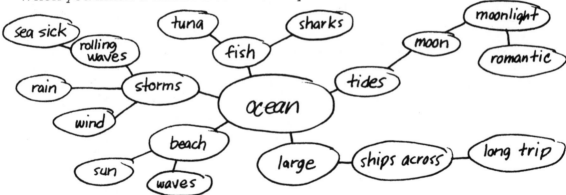

Now, create a cluster for the word "school."

$$\boxed{school}$$

Organizers

Organizers do just what their title implies: they organize information. There are many different types of organizers and they are known by many names and come in many forms: graphic organizers, graphic overviews, clusters, webs, charts, Venn Diagrams, and timelines. Many organizers are named by their purpose, such as cause and effect organizers, topic organizers, and sequence organizers.

Organizers are a useful strategy to help students understand complex information in any content area. They are a visual representation of how text or content is organized. They show the relationships of topics, concepts, and details. Because organizers are visual, many students are better able to grasp how the facts fit together. For instance, a student more readily understands the global nature of World War II when he or she sees an organizer.

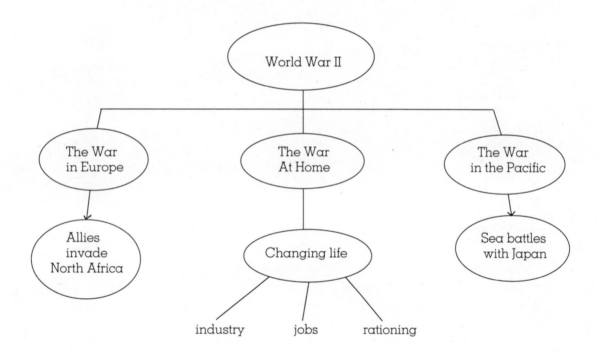

To make students comfortable with organizers, use them throughout the curriculum. They can help students better understand what they are hearing, reading, and writing. A graphic overview can introduce an area of study. A partial or blank organizer can assess a student's knowledge of what they've already studied. Text-structure organizers can show students how the text in a

science book is organized, helping students identify important topics, supporting details, and extraneous facts. They can use a listening organizer for note-taking during a lecture. They can analyze fiction and non-fiction to determine specific text structures; then they can use these to structure their own writing. There are hundreds of organizers and even more uses for them.

In many activities in this book, I suggest one type of organizer or another. In other places, students must make their own choice. It is important for students to make these choices, so that they learn which organizer is best for each specific situation. The following pages discuss some specific organizers that are useful in all content areas and that the students will encounter in this and other books.

Category organizers categorize information. Categorization is a basic thinking skill and can help students identify common traits and compare categories. Several different structures can be used for categorization. A simple structure shows only the categories.

Furniture
tables
beds
chairs

Clothes
dresses
jeans
t-shirts

Buildings
house
office building
bank

More complex category organizers show details about each item. They require students to analyze the category and its members for supporting details.

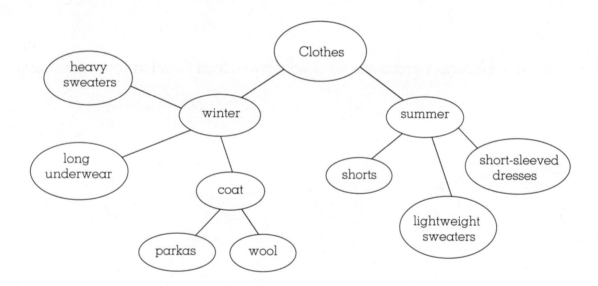

In the activity "Life Was Different Then" (page 66), students list the details of life in a historical period. They create categories and organize the details under them. The organizer can be simple or very complex depending on the student's use of thinking skills. Students then use the same categories to create an organizer about life today. This allows them to compare and contrast life at the two different times, draw conclusions, and form opinions. The organizers clearly show the facts, giving the students food for thought. Without them, many students would have trouble making the transition from facts to personal opinion.

Organizers: CATEGORY ORGANIZERS

Organizers show information in an organization or framework. They help us see how ideas go together. Some organizers categorize words or facts or put details into specific categories. Here's an example.

FOOD GROUPS

MEAT	DAIRY	VEGETABLES	FRUIT
steak	milk	lettuce	apples
bacon	cheese	broccoli	grapes
hot dogs	ice cream	squash	oranges

Create a category organizer for twenty-five things found in your classroom.

Charts are another way of categorizing data. Charts list or compare several things in a simple box form. Charts are usually easy to read, even when complex data is presented. Students should be familiar with charts because of their frequent use in both social studies and science. After creating their own charts, students find the charted information easier to understand. Charts are useful as a note-taking structure, too.

In the activity "Prairie Shark" (page 99), students create their own charts. The headings of the columns are given, but students must fill in the chart with information they either know or locate during their research. They must then evaluate this information, choose a variety of traits, and synthesize them into an imaginary animal.

Name _____ **Date**_____

Like other organizers, charts show information in a clear form and help us see how ideas go together. Here's one example:

	Raccoons	Rabbits
Size	about 3 feet long	under 14 inches long
Food	frogs, fish, eggs, corn nuts, small animals	green, leafy plants, twigs, bark
Activities	hunts at night	eats and plays dusk to dawn
Where live	North and South America	Africa, Europe North and South America, Australia
Interesting facts	strong, skillful fingers good swimmers	if chased can run 18 miles an hour. Depends on sense of smell and hearing

Create a chart that shows what you would find in your classroom and in your room at home.

Compare and contrast organizers force students to observe, analyze, and often evaluate data. They show the similarities and differences between items.

There are several forms of compare and contrast organizers. Some organize the information by listing the traits of the items being compared.

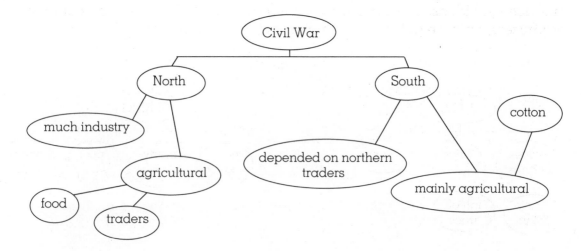

Another compare and contrast organizer is called a "Venn Diagram." It is often used in math to determine sets. Overlapping circles show how two or three items are alike and different. For instance, in the example below, one circle stands for oceans and the other lakes. There are several details in the overlapping section (characteristics that are the same) as well as in each of the separate sections (characteristics which are not shared by both).

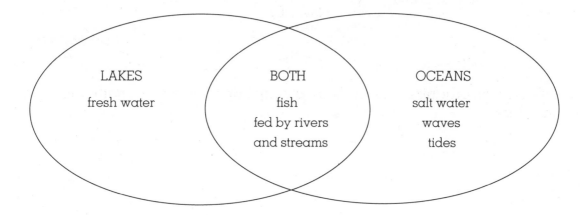

In the activity "Starship Captain's Log" (page 109) students must first research facts about two planets and put these details into chart form. This insures that students know the facts. Then they create a Venn Diagram to compare the planets. The use of the Venn Diagram makes the final writing easier because the data has already been organized to show the individual and shared characteristics.

33

From *The Content Connection*, published by Good Year Books. Copyright © 1991 Hilarie N. Staton.

Name _____   **Date** _____

Organizers show information in an organization or framework. They help us see how ideas go together. They can help us get ready to write by organizing our facts and ideas. Some organizers compare items. Compare and contrast organizers can take different forms. Some simply list details.

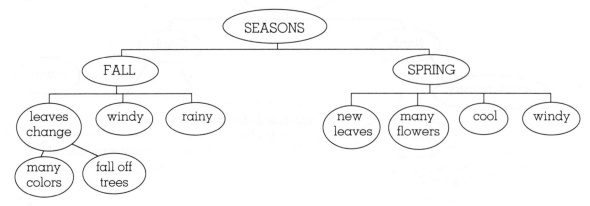

Others are better at showing exactly how things are alike and different:

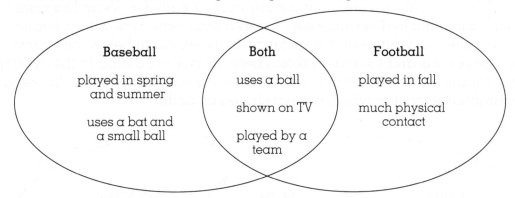

Create an organizer that compares what happens in your math and reading classes.

Sequence is an important aspect in writing. For writers to produce an intelligible recipe, story, or newspaper article, they must pay attention to the sequence of events. Sequential organizers are a good way to keep details clear and in order.

A timeline is one simple sequence organizer. This one is about the events in *Charlotte's Web*.

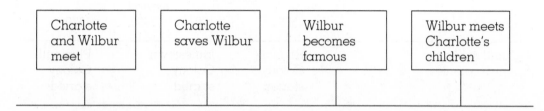

Organizers can become very complex when you add details, minor events and tangents. You choose the complexity when you create the organizer.

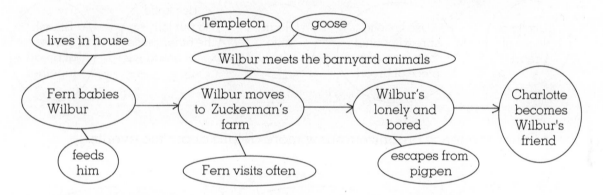

Some sequential organizers give the steps in a process or cycle, such as the steps in an experiment or in the life cycle of a moth.

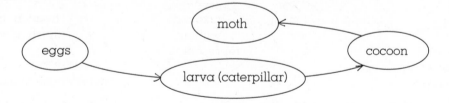

Students find sequential organizers useful for many purposes and in every content area. Complex events can be clarified with either very simple or more detailed sequential organizers. Because these organizers show a sequence with few words, they are easy to follow and to create. To create them, students must analyze, sequence, and interpret the facts. They can write an organizer for topics as diverse as a historical event or the steps in a math process.

The activity "A Day at a Time," (page 81) has students analyze a story by creating a sequential, problem-solving organizer. Then they use the sequence as the basis for diary entries from the point of view of a specific character.

Name _____   **Date** _____

Organizers show information in an organization or framework. Some organizers show the order in which things are done or the order in which events happened. A timeline is one type of sequence organizer.

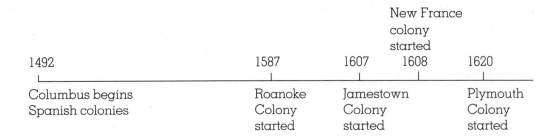

New France colony started

1492		1587	1607	1608	1620

Columbus begins Spanish colonies

Roanoke Colony started

Jamestown Colony started

Plymouth Colony started

Other sequence organizers show the order in which things have to be done.

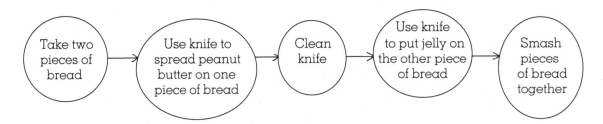

Take two pieces of bread → Use knife to spread peanut butter on one piece of bread → Clean knife → Use knife to put jelly on the other piece of bread → Smash pieces of bread together

Other sequence organizers show more details about the events.

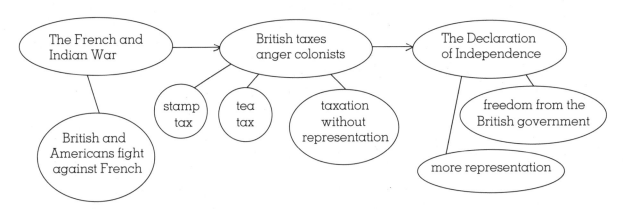

The French and Indian War → British taxes anger colonists → The Declaration of Independence

British and Americans fight against French

stamp tax

tea tax

taxation without representation

freedom from the British government

more representation

Create a sequence organizer that shows five things that have happened to you during your life.

Organizers:
CAUSE & EFFECT
ORGANIZERS

Cause and effect organizers are a type of sequential organizer. Arrows are used to show the direction of the action (from cause to effect). Simple ones show one cause and its effect.

More complex organizers show many causes or many effects.

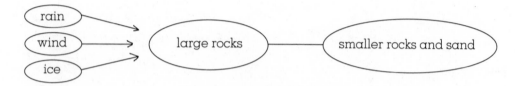

Other organizers give details about the causes or effects.

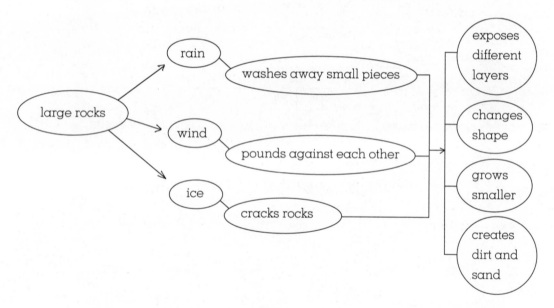

Since they show cause and effect so clearly, you can use these cause and effect organizers to simplify complex relationships in any content area. They can help students understand such diverse problems as pollution, mysteries, human motivation, or governmental actions. As with all sequential organizers, they show the sequence with a few words, but cause and effect organizers require more data analysis and interpretation to develop.

In the activity "Garbage, Smog, and Acid Rain" (page 107), students use cause and effect organizers to brainstorm and analyze different types of pollution. They must analyze facts from prior knowledge and outside resources to create a simple and then a complex organizer. The details from the complex organizer are used to form and support their opinion about that type of pollution.

Name _____   Date_____

Organizers show information in a framework. One organizer, called a "cause and effect organizer," helps us see causes and effects clearly. The effect is the event that happened. The causes tell why that event happened. These organizers help us get ready to write about causes (why it happened) and effects (what happened). Sometimes they show:

one cause and one effect

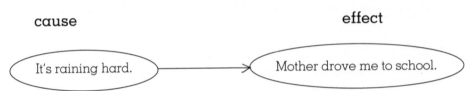

cause   effect

It's raining hard. → Mother drove me to school.

or many causes that lead to one effect

causes   effect

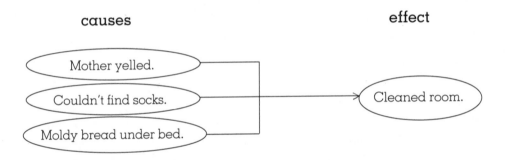

Mother yelled.
Couldn't find socks. → Cleaned room.
Moldy bread under bed.

or even many causes that lead to many effects.

causes   effects

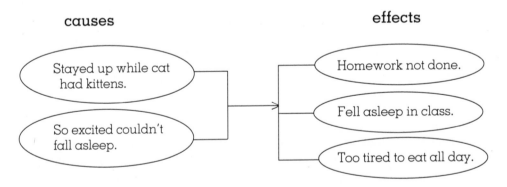

Stayed up while cat had kittens.   Homework not done.
So excited couldn't fall asleep. →   Fell asleep in class.
                                                    Too tired to eat all day.

Create an organizer that shows the causes and effects of someone who is unhappy.

A "topic organizer" revolves around a topic, word, or phrase, and it is similar to a cluster. Some topic organizers show an overview of a topic (a structured overview) while introducing key terms and the relationships between important facts and concepts.

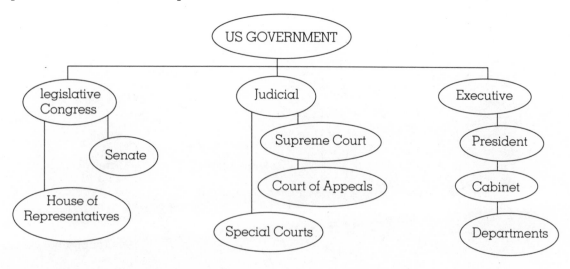

Overviews such as these can be used to introduce units, chapters, or concepts. They relate students' prior knowledge to the new information and help students make the connections between what has already been studied and what's to be studied next. Creating this type of organizer demands detailed data analysis and interpretation, as well as sequencing, classification, and other thinking skills.

Open-ended topic organizers are less specific. They use general topics around which specific data can be arranged. They are especially useful as a framework for research and note-taking. I've used open-ended organizers in this book so students can have as much freedom as possible in choosing their topics.

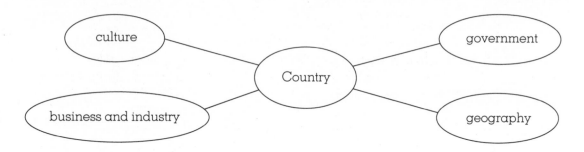

In the activity, "And On Your Left . . ." (page 142) students use an open-ended topic organizer as the framework for their research about a region. As they add details to the organizer, students can easily see where they need more facts. Later they can choose those facts that are pertinent to the writing assignment.

Name _____   **Date** _____

Organizers show information in an organization or framework. they help us see how ideas go together. Topic organizers arrange information around a topic. Sometimes the information is given to us:

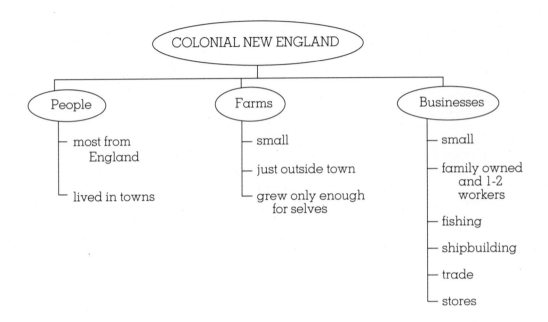

Other times an organizer consists of just the basic framework, and we have to add the details. After it's complete, the facts will be organized around the chosen topic.

This organizer is just a framework. Use it while you do research on an animal.

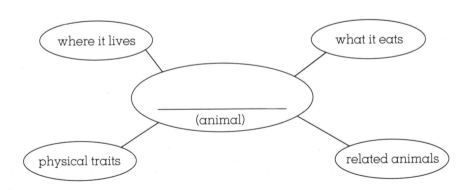

Organizers: TEXT - STRUCTURE ORGANIZERS

The final type of organizer is a text-structure organizer. This type deals with the way the text is organized. It is a visual representation of an outline you might create for a piece you're writing or something you've read. When a student creates a text-structure organizer for a writing assignment, he or she can see more clearly how to organize their final work.

This organizer will work for any type of assignment. For example, if the text is to be a compare and contrast piece, the organizer might look like this:

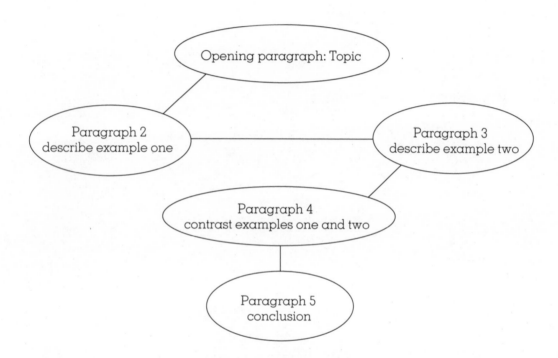

Text-structure organizers are especially helpful for students whose writing is disorganized or who panic when they must answer essay questions. For instance, if an essay question asks a compare and contrast question, the student can recall the structure above and then concentrate on placing the content information on the framework. When they begin writing, everything is already organized, and they can concentrate on putting the pertinent facts into sentences. As students become more confident, they can change the organization, but at least they have a place to start.

Below are ideas for several more text-structure organizers. Many are just basic organizers that can be related to specific key words. By teaching them as skeletons on which to hang the facts, you can help students become more confident in their writing.

Although their use is not required, text-structure organizers can be used for many of the assignments in this book.

Opinion or Persuasion Organizer:

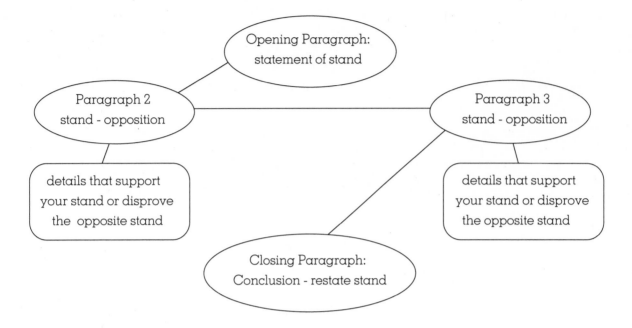

Cause and Effect Organizer:

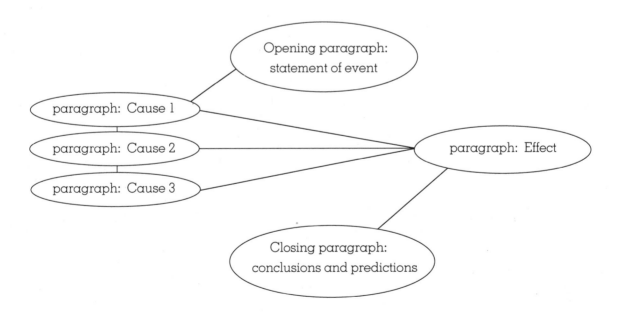

Name _____   **Date** _____

Discuss a Controversial Issue:

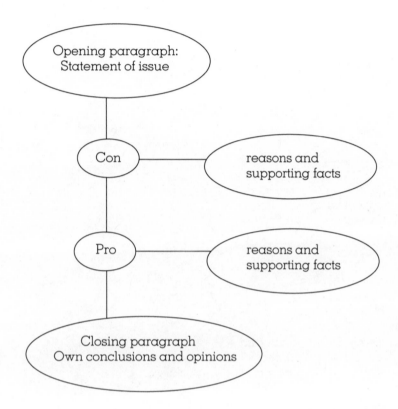

Organizers: TEXT-STRUCTURE ORGANIZERS

Organizers show information in an organization or framework. A text-structure organizer helps organize our facts and ideas in the form we will write. A different type of organizer is used for each different type of writing.

To get ready to write a compare-contrast essay about bears, you can use a compare-contrast organizer like the one below. Each circle will become a paragraph when we write the essay.

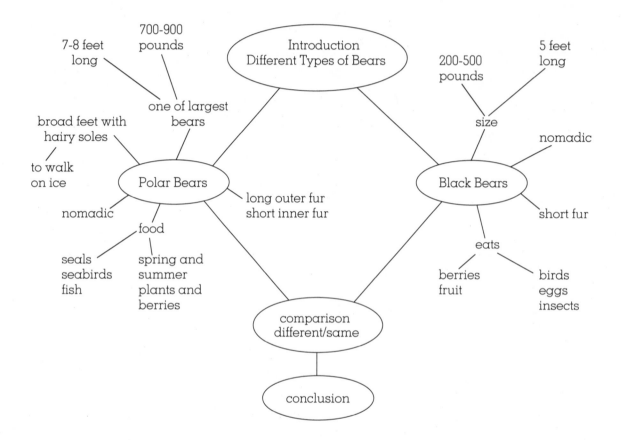

Write an essay about two places you like. Before you write, create a compare-contrast organizer, like the one above, with your details.

The Writing Phase
▼

The writing step is the rush to put down the thoughts, phrases, and ideas that have been stirred up by the pre-writing activities. It is only one step, and if students understand that, they are less threatened by the prospect of putting the words to paper.

During pre-writing, the writer has thought about ideas; played with these ideas by organizing them and relating them to other ideas; noted interesting words and phrases; and become excited by the prospect of communicating these ideas to others. Writing is the step where everything done during the pre-writing step comes together. Some writers find it the easiest step and others find it the hardest. Some find it rewarding and others find it frustrating. You will meet some of each kind when you teach. Remember, writers at this step, like all the other steps, need careful nurturing and much encouragement.

As writers rush to put their ideas down on the page, they should not be hindered by the correction of minor errors or even major ones. This first draft, or "sloppy copy," will be corrected later. Perfection is not needed because the writing still has to go through revising, editing, and publishing.

This doesn't mean revisions and editing can't go on while you write, just that the corrections shouldn't slow the flow of ideas. When I write, I make corrections and revisions as I go, but I never stop the flow of thoughts to make major changes. If I need more facts while writing or if I realize something is not clear, I mark it and return to it during my revision. If students hit a "writer's block" (and we all do), suggest they discuss their content with a peer or with you. Often this frees thoughts and the ideas are soon flowing again. The writing step has its own reward—seeing your thoughts on paper.

Those students who have trouble understanding and using different types of writing forms might be helped by a strategy called a "frame." Frames give the student a specific writing structure and key words in a form they can use as their own. Frames contain blank lines and key words. Students write details about the topic, and they are encouraged to write more than one sentence in appropriate blanks. They get the feel for the organization and soon feel confident enough to use the form without the frame. The key words creep into their writing in the right places.

Use the following frame to help students understand how to write directions:

To make a _____ , first you _____

Then you _____

Be careful that _____

Finally you _____

If it is a good one, you can _____

A frame for comparing two books allows the students to see the structure and key words necessary to any compare and contrast writing. This frame is specifically written for the topic, but others can be more general.

I just read the book_____ by

_____. Another book about a

similar_____ is _____

by _____.

These books are similar because _____

_____

_____

_____

These books are different because _____

_____

_____

_____

In my opinion, _____

_____

_____

_____

_____

Although no story frames are used in this book, they can be developed for most of the activities. For instance, a frame for the activity "A Scientist's Opinion" (page 95) might look like this:

I believe the _____ should be nominated for Animal of the Year.

It is special in many ways. It lives _____

For food it _____

_____

It has been seen _____

_____

When it sees people, it _____

_____

My opinion is _____

because of these facts _____

_____

Frames are a step toward independence, but for some students, a very necessary step. They allow students successes without forcing them to take risks beyond their capabilities. Frames are a modeling technique from which students go on to improved independent writing.

Once students have a first draft, they take the next step: working with that draft to make it the best and clearest writing possible.

The Revising and Editing Phase
▼

Editing and revising are often considered one step, although they are done as two. In revising, the structure and meaning are fixed; in editing, the mechanics, grammar, and spelling are fixed. Writers should do both before they create the final copy.

After the first draft is complete, the writer begins the revising process. He or she checks the writing for meaning, structure, and language. The student determines how the writing can be made more interesting or how a better flow can be created or if the main ideas are supported by facts. For teachers, revising consists of encouraging writers to improve their work, now, while they're still in the writing process, before the evaluation and grading.

Students should understand the purpose of this step and realize that it is their chance to get help and to solve problems. Neither their peers nor the teacher is evaluating their writing; rather, they are trying to help the student create a better final product. This step provides an excellent learning situation because isolated skills are fit into a useful context. Learning here is much more meaningful than correcting later. After all, how many students learn from those little notes in red on the paper they turned in a week ago?

Teachers have to be judicious in the use of revision. It doesn't need to be done on every assignment, only on those that are to be shared or "published." Writing that is to be handed in and forgotten or has no real potential should end with the first draft.

Since revision is hard work, many students see it as punishment. They must see proof that it is worth the time and trouble. Proof often comes in the form of pride, grades, or publishing praise. One way to encourage revision is to require the first draft and the final product to be turned in. Evaluate both for changes and growth, not just whether the final product is correct.

For students, revising usually consists of their own revisions, a peer conference, and a teacher conference. After reading their first draft, writers make the obvious changes they feel improve their writing.

Peer conferences can be done with a partner or a small group. Classes need to "grow into" peer conferences. Individuals need to develop both the confidence and the necessary skills. They need training in how to listen to others, in how to praise, and in how to identify problems. As they learn these skills, their comments become more complex and they become better evaluators.

The writer reads his or her paper to a revision partner or group. The responders use a teacher-created response sheet to determine what they will discuss. A response sheet makes sure the questions are appropriate to the assignment and that important skills are covered. All conferences should begin with what is good or what the responder likes about the writing. In early conferences, responders also might ask a question about the information or structure (see Sample 1, page 50). As students develop better listening and thinking skills, their questions become more specific (see Sample 2). They can ask about the structure or the amount of details or dialogue, or they can identify tangents or irrelevant information. As students progress, the questions will become more sophisticated and specific (see Sample 3).

Each response sheet should contain only a few important questions that reflect the teacher's objectives. Questions can be about the writer's purpose, organization, language, or style. Examine the content of the questions for clarity, relevancy, and interest. If students are writing for a special audience, such as kindergarten students, include questions about whether the language is appropriate to that audience. Students can use these response sheets for their own revisions, as well as part of the teacher's revising conference.

Both formal and informal teacher conferences should occur throughout the writing process. During these conferences, the writer responds to the teacher's questions, suggestions, and impressions. Trust is what makes a productive conference. However, it takes time for trust between a teacher and a student to develop, especially if students are not used to the teacher being a guiding rather than a grading force. Conferences are not the time for grades, but rather a time for suggestions and guidance.

Hold the teacher revision conference before the student creates the final copy. Students should realize that you are not evaluating their writing yet, but helping them perfect their final product. Zero in on one or two main problems that stem from the assignment's objectives or from student weaknesses. Your questions during the conference may reflect the same concerns as the revision sheets. They can help students expand or clarify their ideas; gain a better understanding of the writing process; or reshape the structure of their writing. If you ask questions instead of telling students what is wrong, they will be forced to clarify their thinking rather than to defend their writing. As this happens, students identify weak spots and can make appropriate changes. For example, if a student is writing about a planet and has left out a description of its atmosphere, ask about it. Once they tell you the information, have them decide if it should be included in their writing.

After the revision conferences, students need time to think about the suggestions that were made by both peers and the teacher. They need to make a conscious decision whether or not to use each suggestion, and they should be able to defend their decision. Students should not hesitate to mark up their copy. They need to understand that the working copy is separate from the final product. It is a step toward a more perfect product.

After they have revised the meaning, structure, and content, students must look at the mechanics of writing. Peer conferences, teacher conferences, and check lists are often used for editing. A few recurring or newly learned skills should be emphasized, as well as standard mechanical and grammar rules. Students may need individual attention to remediate problem areas or to extend information from class lessons.

Both revising and editing sheets should reflect those areas the teacher will use in the final evaluation. Revising and editing are learning steps where isolated skills become meaningful and the writing is tested for its ability to communicate meaning.

Sample 1 Simple Response Sheet (for "Facts of Life," page 94)

What I liked best about this script:

An interesting fact was:

A question I have about the information:

_____

Sample 2 Middle Response Sheet (for "In the Eyes of the Beholder," page 131)

What specific things were interesting about the diary entries?

What questions do you have about the differences in what the people saw?

Where would you add more details?

_____

Sample 3 Complex Response Sheet (for "You are There!," page 80)

What specific things were good about the news story?

What questions do you have about the event?

Were all the details relevant to the story?

Where would you use more interesting details?

Editing question: Are the correct verb tenses used throughout the story?

Sample Questions for a Response Group

Does the writer stick to the topic or go off in many directions?

Is the writer trying to cover too much or too little?

Is it easy to understand?

Are there parts you found confusing?

Are there places with not enough or too many details?

Can you visualize the people, places, and action?

Is it interesting?

Are there parts you thought were out of order?

Does the beginning introduce the subject and point of view?

Is the ending exciting?

Is the writing too simple or too hard for the audience?

How could the author communicate better with this particular audience?

Are hard words explained or defined?

Are the main points supported by enough facts?

Is the climax exciting? Does it make sense in relation to the
    rest of the events?

Does the writer support his opinions with facts?

Does the writer need more explanation?

Can you suggest any good arguments or facts for the author to use?

Sample Questions for Teacher-Writer Revision Conferences

Who is your audience and how have you written just for them?

From whose point of view is the story told? How can a reader tell that?

Why is this section important to the topic?

What is the main idea of your article?

How do these facts relate to the main idea?

Which is your best description? Why is it better than the others?

Are the descriptions of your characters and setting important to the story?

What question might a kindergartner have after hearing this story?

In what order do the events happen?

Can your ideas be arranged in a different way?

What is your opinion? What facts support it?

Is your audience going to understand the technical words you use?

Sample Specific Content Questions

What is life like for your characters? Where can you add some of these details to your story?

Why do you think your experiment had these results?

Does the character you are interviewing sound like the one in the book?

Sample Teacher Revision Conference Questions
(for "Dinosaur Zoo," page 102)

What is special about this dinosaur? Did you include this in your letter?

Can you match each of your suggestions or opinions with a supporting fact?

Will the zookeeper have enough information to get the zoo ready for the dinosaur?

Editing Questions:

Did you use the proper form for a business letter and include capital letters in the correct places?

Have you checked the spelling of technical words?

The Final Step: The Final Copy
Publishing and Evaluation
▼

After the revising and editing stage, students must create a final copy of the work. They must copy their work in the best possible form, proofread it, and add any necessary illustrations. Some students may need help in creating a final copy of which they are proud. Teach them to use a word processor or enlist the help of parents or volunteers as typists. Help each child create a quality presentation.

Not all assignments need a final copy or to be published. Many can end before this stage. Students need practice in all of the steps of the writing process, and while they are practicing there is no need to force them to "publish" their attempts. Only those assignments identified as the student's best work by both the writer and the teacher need be shared with the "public." However, every student should have many opportunities to experience the joy and personal accomplishment that comes with publishing.

If the assignment ends before this step, often the only audience is the teacher. But many assignments should go on to be published (in other words, to be read by a larger audience). Publishing is the true evaluation of writing. Writers always want to know how the audience responds. It tells us how well we've communicated our ideas. Students need to see a variety of people—their classmates, families, younger students, other schools, adults, and businesses—responding to their work.

Publishing can take many forms. Class collections, such as newspapers or books, can be shared with other classes, next year's class, or other schools. Posters, picture books, class displays, and the oral presentation of reports and plays are all ways students can share their writing. They can mail letters to a real person, like an author, politician, or celebrity, or students can write letters to fictional or historical figures. The answers can be written by classmates, who respond to the letters as if they were the addressee. PTA bulletins, magazines that publish children's writing, and businesses are "real world" audience for students' writing.

Finally, the teacher evaluates the student's product; he or she does not correct the work. If the teacher has kept in touch with the student's writing throughout the process, most corrections have already been made. What the teacher determines now is how well the paper fulfills the assignment's objectives. If the teacher has shared the assignment objectives and evaluation criteria with students, and has used them as part of student-teacher conferences (both formal and informal), then students can probably predict what their evaluation will be.

Teachers must limit what they expect. Since the purpose of writing is communicating, a paper should be evaluated on whether it communicates the required information. That is the first and foremost criteria. Do not accept anything just because it is creative; only accept pieces that make sense within the structure given or chosen by the writer. Ask questions like: Is it clearly and interestingly presented? Are the facts and conclusions correct? Do the facts fit the topic?

Although the use of specified techniques, forms, and grammar are secondary to the content, they are not forgotten. Not every minor rule should be evaluated, only those stressed during the writing process. Each writing form will have specific criteria that need to be evaluated: whether the heading in a letter is present, whether there are enough supporting details, whether the language is appropriate to the form, and whether the appropriate organization has been used. Usage and mechanics should be part of the evaluation, too, but they should not be the major portion of it. If we are asking students to think and communicate with their writing, then the handwriting, grammar, and spelling are not our main objectives.

As we evaluate papers, new problems come to light. These should become the basis for future lessons and the next writing assignment's objectives and revision sheets.

Careful thought and creativity join to create writing that must meet specific standards. We set these standards, sometimes for individuals, more often for the class, and then show students how to reach them. We require that students strive to reach these standards time after time. We evaluate how well they do and when they achieve it comfortably, we raise the standards, so students are continually growing. Writing is a process that can be used in any content area. When nurtured, it provides amazing growth in thinking skills, creativity, and knowledge.

Students with Writing Problems

Many students, including those with learning disabilities, have serious problems with writing. They can't think of what to write, and when they finally decide, they don't write very much. What they write is disorganized, sloppy, and has no relevance to the topic. We've all had students with these problems. Here are a few suggestions that might make life easier for some of them—and us.

1. Begin with informal writing. Personal journals give them a chance to write about their favorite topics. They learn they don't need to fear correction or censure, but they do have to communicate their ideas. They learn to express their thoughts clearly, so that the reader will understand what they are trying to say. They also are forced to write something—and that is often half the battle. When students are ready, introduce learning logs or assign focused free writing activities. These allow them to write about specific content topics before they must write for an audience. Remember, some students progress very slowly and the progress in their informal writing does not show up immediately in their more structured writing.

2. When working with a group of slower or LD students, you can't assume they understand how you got from point A to point B in your thinking. Tell them exactly what you were thinking. Tell them what your thoughts were and which ideas you discarded and why. Do more Language Experience writing with them, for through these models students will learn exactly what they are supposed to do.

3. Adapt writing assignments to give them the supports they need to experience success and to learn the skills necessary for more structured writing. Spend more time making sure they understand the assignment's requirements and the necessary content. Before writing about a topic, students should talk about the information. Have them explain what they know to a peer or to you or carry on a class discussion (but be sure they participate). They will surprise themselves with what they know and will be more confident about the content when they sit down to write. They also need to discuss the assignment. Hold a conference before they begin the pre-writing activities or between the pre-writing and writing steps. Have them describe their plans for the assignment and possibly list their plans, so they can keep track of what they need to do and what they've already done.

4. These students need to be taught many strategies we don't usually teach in depth. Model how a strategy is used, and then give the students structured practice. Be sure they use the strategy every time it is appropriate—in every content class. Many of these students don't transfer what they learn, so it is imperative that they hear the same terms (such as pre-writing, organizer, revising) in every class. This is the only way to teach them to generalize what they learn. We all know a remedial reader who can "find the main idea" perfectly with the reading teacher, but not in social studies class.

5. Limit what is expected of these students. Eliminate writing steps for some assignments; not everything has to go through the revision process. Where we might expect regular students to take their own notes, these students might need a structure (outline or organizer) with clues on it. Headings, key words, and the organization of the lecture or reading can help them take more appropriate notes. If your main objective is to see what the students know about a topic, give them a blank text-structure organizer on which they can take their notes. Then teach them how to write from it so it becomes the organization of their writing. If your goal is to have them use a new writing form independently, have them write about a topic that requires fewer higher level thinking skills.

6. Sometimes individuals and groups do not progress as we expect. Don't be afraid to go back to modeling or Language Experience activities. Instead of assigning individual writing assignments, have small groups carry out pre-writing activities and then have individuals write from those activities. At other times you might give them a completed organizer and have them write from that.

7. Have students do their writing in class. Class writing time will allow you time to conference, evaluate, and guide their work. This is also an excellent way to keep the procrastinator moving. Since they are working with the content, we shouldn't feel guilty when they are writing in science class. Remember when writing is done with the content, it is understood better and remembered longer, so there is probably more learning going on than if we lectured or gave a reading assignment.

8. Revising and editing can present problems to these students, so give them limited, but detailed, lists of what to look for. If you personalize these lists, you can include the student's particular weaknesses and eliminate the skills they have mastered. For instance, a student who writes simple sentences correctly might not need "capitals" and "periods" on their editing sheet, but they might need "various sentence forms" on their revision sheet. Use the same evaluation sheet for the student, the peer conference, and the teacher revision conference. That way the final copy will reflect the student's progress in handling these specific skills.

9. Be sure these students publish their work often. However, the time spent and the tension created in trying to get a perfect copy isn't always worth the result. For some students, you may have to make the published copy yourself or teach them how to use the computer's word processing capabilities. A typed copy looks published and the errors don't glare. The pride students feel in seeing others reading and responding to their work help motivate them for the next writing assignment.

10. Limit your final evaluation criteria to just a few important skills. Tailor them to fit the individual needs of each student. Be sure students know what will be expected of them so that they are not trying to perfect everything at once. At first, these goals should be well within their abilities. Later you can raise these standards, so both you and the student see progress. Keep some of their papers so that they can identify their progress. We all forget how badly we did at something when we were first learning it.

The writing process is not beyond these students. They just need guidance to master it. We have to provide the appropriate guidance if we expect them to succeed.

CONTENT AREA *Activities*

The purpose of this book is to: make life a little easier for teachers; give them some new ideas; and provide students with enjoyable, creative and meaningful lessons. The activities in this book link thinking and writing skills to science, social studies, and literature. They are not designed to teach content, but to force the students to use content in new and different ways. All of them involve the use of complex thinking skills and challenging writing assignments.

When you're planning a geology lesson or a history review, it is not always easy to come up with a writing assignment that uses specific thinking skills and also challenges and interests students. This book is filled with writing lessons that expand thinking skills by having students do unusual and creative writing assignments in those content areas normally taught in grades four through eight. The activities can be used "as is" or adapted for use with different subjects.

The chart on pages 61–63 details some of the thinking skills required for each lesson. All the lessons require reporting facts, so this skill is not listed. The remaining thinking skills fall into the categories of interpreting data, analyzing data (categorizing, cause and effect, compare and contrast, sequence), synthesis, evaluation, critical thinking, creative thinking, and problem solving. These categories are an easy way to analyze the thinking skills, but not the only way. The list is not inclusive and unlisted skills are often required.

The topics covered in this book are found in most fourth-, fifth-, and sixth-grade elementary English, social studies, and science curricula. Content is not taught during the lessons, so students should already be familiar with the topic. Research is encouraged and often required.

Some of the lessons are relatively simple and can be used with gifted third and most fourth graders. Other lessons are more appropriate to older elementary or middle school students. Most lessons can be adapted for less able students by adding more teacher guidance in the pre-writing phase or by doing a class example which follows the procedure.

The lessons in this book follow the basic writing process: pre-writing, writing, and revising and editing. Publishing is left up to the teacher. The activities do place extra emphasis on the pre-writing "Thinking and Organizing" stage, where students use a variety of methods to find information (real or imaginary, facts or feelings) and organize it (clustering, listing, etc.). Some students may want to substitute clusters for lists or do organizers where none are required. Encourage students to use techniques with which they are comfortable—as long as they use the higher level thinking skills.

Students use their pre-writing information in a variety of writing formats: letters, reports, journals, speeches, scripts, and stories. Refer back to the pre-writing section for possible organizing techniques. Encourage students to be creative and adapt the activities to their own needs and interests.

After students finish their writing, they should revise and edit with specific content and skills in mind. Sometimes they can use an "editing audience," such as a classmate. Encourage students to publish and share their finished product.

Adapting Activities

These activities can be used during social studies, science, health, literature, or English lessons. They can be used when teaching a writing form or during a content unit. You can assign the science activity "Baying Like a Foghorn" (page 97) during an English class on poetry or similes and metaphors or during a science class on a particular animal.

Some activities will need introduction by way of a lesson. For the science activity "Alien Zoo" (page 108), students need to know how plants and animals adapt to their environment. Other activities, such as "Like an Unopened Book" (page 143) can be used in learning centers or as individual assignments.

The activities can be adapted in 1001 ways. You can substitute different writing forms, such as a journal entry or radio show instead of a letter. The pre-writing and writing concepts can be applied to other content subjects. The health lesson "Ker-choo, Again" (page 121) becomes a social studies lesson when students write a children's book about the causes and effects of an important historical event, such as the building of the Erie Canal. Literature lessons can be done with historical characters or geographical settings. General lessons, such as the science lesson "All the News!" (page 117), can be limited to a specific area of study, such as weather. The variations are endless.

The Activity Chart

The chart on pages 61–63 lists the content, thinking skills, and writing form in each lesson. Many of the activities are interdisciplinary and cover several subjects areas but are listed only under the major content topic. The major thinking skills are listed, although the use of other skills may be required. The chart allows you to locate lessons quickly to fit your immediate needs. At the front of each content section is a short section suggesting ways to use writing, specifically these activities, in the content classroom.

Activity Chart

Name	Content	Thinking Skills	Writing Form
Life Was Different Then	Literature: Setting	classification, compare-contrast evaluation	letter
A Wonderful Place	Literature: Setting	analyze data, creative thinking	short story
The Scene, The Setting, The Place	Literature: Setting	categorization, critical thinking	tour speech
What a Visit!	Literature: Setting	sequence, synthesis creative thinking	story
Full of Fillers	Literature: Setting	analyze data, critical thinking	filler
Like an Eagle in the Sky	Literature: Characters	evaluation, imagery	description
Pooh Bear Meets Mary Poppins	Literature: Characters	compare-contrast, critical thinking, creative thinking	letter
And What Do You Think of. . .	Literature: Characters	interpret data synthesis	magazine interview
Poetic Feelings	Literature: Characters	interpret data, creative thinking	poem
Dear Robin Hood	Literature: Characters	creative thinking, evaluation	letter
Everybody's Got Problems	Literature: Characters	critical thinking, problem solving	advice column
You Are There!	Literature: Plot	analyze data, creative thinking	radio news report
A Day at a Time	Literature: Plot	analyze data, synthesis	diary
Just Because It's Not in Print. . .	Literature: Plot	interpret data creative thinking	essay
Camera, Action	Literature: Plot	classification interpret data	television or movie script
From Another Point of View	Literature: Point of View	analyze data, creative thinking	scene
From Your Editor	Literature: Evaluating Literature	critical thinking problem solving	letter
Words, Words, and More Words	Literature: Vocabulary	interpret data, synthesis	vocabulary test
Movie Madness	Literature: Movie Preferences	fact-opinion, critical thinking	movie review

Activity Chart

Name	Content	Thinking Skills	Writing Form
Books Open the World	Literature: Preferences	categorization, evaluation	speech
Facts of Life	Science: Animals	classification, creative thinking	television script
A Scientist's Option	Science: Animals	fact-opinion, evaluation	report
Baying Like a Foghorn	Science: Animals	compare-contrast imagery, creative thinking	poem
A Prairie Shark	Science: Animals	compare-contrast, creative thinking	scientific article
Godzilla on Broadway	Science: Animals	synthesis, creative thinking	story
Dinosaur Zoo	Science: Dinosaurs	interpret data, creative thinking	letter
The Skeleton Talks	Science: Human Body	cause-effect, creative thinking	journal
Like a Rose or a Petunia or a Weed	Science: Plants	categorization synthesis	essay
Purple Mountain's Majesty	Science: Environment, Geology	cause-effect, persuasion	monologue
Garbage, Smog, and Acid Rain	Science: Environment, Pollution	cause-effect persuasion	editorial
Alien Zoo	Science: Planets, Environment	compare-contrast synthesis, creative thinking	letter
Starship Captain's Log	Science: Planets	interpreting data, compare-contrast, evaluation	journal
Science-tionary	Science: Understanding Scientific Terms	interpreting data synthesis	technical dictionary
The Sky is Like the Ocean	Science: Understanding Scientific Terms	compare-contrast, critical thinking	paragraphs
Step-by-Step	Science: Experiment	sequence, cause-effect	experiment
Analyzing a Machine	Science: Simple Machines	cause-effect, evaluation	scientific report
All the News!	Science: Natural Phenomena	cause-effect, critical thinking	newspaper article
Life's a Cycle	Science: The Life Cycle	sequence, sythesis	report

Activity Chart

Name	Content	Thinking Skills	Writing Form
Ker-choo, Again	Health: Prevention	cause-effect, creative thinking	picture book
Helping the World's Children	Health: Prevention	cause-effect evaluation, problem solving	speech
An Apple a Day	Health: Nutrition	interpret data, evaluation	report
Dear Editor, Safety First	Health: Safety	fact-opinion, persuasion	editorial
Crash! Thud! Ow!	Health: Safety	cause-effect, persuasion	speech
Home from the Frontier	Social Studies: Early Settlement	sequence, fact-opinion, synthesis	friendly letter
In the Eyes of the Beholder	Social Studies: Historical Way-of-Life	compare-contrast point-of-view	diary
The Not-So-Perfect Past	Social Studies: Historical Way-of-Life	critical thinking persuasion	editorial
If Only You Knew	Social Studies: Famous Americans	cause-effect creative thinking	letter
A Marvelous Miracle	Social Studies: Technology and Historical Change	sequence, synthesis persuasion	advertisements
Don't Forget the Toothbrushes	Social Studies: Future Communities	categorization, analyze data creative thinking	report
Corn, Cabins, and Carriages	Social Studies: Historical Communities	analyze data creative thinking	story
Armchair Traveler	Social Studies: World Cultures	classification, critical thinking	television travel show
Planning a Vacation?	Social Studies: World Cultures	interpret data, analyze data	magazine artcle
And On Your Left. . .	Social Studies: World Regions	interpreting data, synthesis	tour speech
Like an Unopened Book	Social Studies: Personal Development	compare-contrast prediction	letter to self

Literature

As teachers, we want students to enjoy many forms of literature. But for them to appreciate any literature fully, they must interact with it, and writing is one way to accomplish that. They can use the literature they read as a model or as a jumping-off point for a variety of writing assignments.

As with any subject, writing can help students integrate literature into their own world and to clarify their thoughts. As they think about the book, its ideas, the author, and the story, they manipulate the information and integrate it into what they already know. In other words, they use thinking skills as they perform the task. They can classify the book by type, by their opinion, or by author. They can analyze stories for character, place, and setting. They can evaluate the book for accuracy, interest, and excitement. They can interpret the data to use in other ways, like prediction, imagining themselves in the story or creating their own imaginary world. As they write about the literature, they defend their feelings, choices, and opinions with facts from the literature.

Informal writing about literature can be done in a literature log or response journal. The student and teacher can carry on a written conversation in the log, while the student is reading the text or after it is completed. This allows the teacher to ask focus questions that apply to that book, but not necessarily to those books other students are reading. Through these questions students can identify important plot points, the development of specific character traits, or the way an author describes a setting. The questions can bring details to their attention or require complex thinking skills, such as prediction or synthesis. A plot, character, or setting can be compared to the things within the student's life, to real places, and to other stories or sources.

The techniques described in the pre-writing section of this book can be used to get students thinking about the relationships, sequences, and characters that they encounter in books and stories. They can be used to clarify the confusing or to expand on what they have read. Clusters can help students expose their feelings about the literature, a character, or a setting. Sequence organizers help them keep track of complex events. Topic organizers help organize complex information from non-fiction books. Other organizers can show the relationships between characters. And, of course, any type of organizer can be used as a step in the writing process.

Almost any writing form can be used to write about literature. For instance, in the activity "The Scene, The Setting, The Plot" (page 69), students develop a tour of the setting. In the activity "And What Do You Think of . . . " (page 75), students interview a fictional character. In other activities, students write letters (to and about characters), poems, advice columns, news broadcasts, and television scripts. All these activities are based on literature they have read. The list on page 65 suggests other forms and ways to use them.

Students can publish and share their writing in a number of ways. Their articles, reviews, interviews, and reports can be used to entice other students to read these books. Students can mail letters to the authors (but don't expect individual answers if you send one author a letter from every member of the

Literature

class). Other students can take the role of the author, a character, or an editor to write an answer.

Writing and literature should be inseparable. Literature gives students enjoyment, sparks their imagination, and gives them a model and a subject to write about. As they play with their own words, they gain a greater appreciation for authors and more confidence as one.

Ideas for Literature Writing Assignments

journals or diaries: of a character; of reader's thoughts while reading; to a character

biographies: of a character; of an author

letters: to a character; character to character (across books or within one book); to review a book; to an editor (persuasive); to an author (critique, praise)

poems: about a character, setting, event, book

radio plays or video scripts: recreate or continue an event; interview a character; a news broadcast from an event

stories: further adventures of a character; adventures of minor characters; what happens when the student meets a character; from the point of view of an inanimate object within a story

picture books: introduce a character; simplify events of the story; organize and report facts

newspapers or magazines
    articles: report events; review or describe the book; fillers; tabloid articles; travel articles about the setting; comparisons of several similar books
    editorials: about events or a concept from the book
    interviews: with an author; others who have read the book; or with the book's characters

dictionaries: important or unfamiliar vocabulary from the book

debates: possible solutions to the problems of a character; results of an action taken; moral dilemma

research reports: about the author; about information from details in the book (such as how hogs are actually raised after reading *Charlotte's Web*); about the setting (such as about the historical period), events or characters in book; about basic scientific facts book uses (such as time travel)

Literature: SETTING

Life Was Different Then

Think & Organize Read a novel or short story that takes place at another time in history. Create a list of details from the story that show that it does not take place in the present. For example, if you've chosen *The Witch of Blackbird Pond*, you might list: fire for heat and cooking, slaves, and stew in wooden bowls.

Title of Novel or Story:

Details:

Organize your list into categories, like food, school, jobs, and homes.
    Think about how life has changed since your story took place. Make an organizer with the same categories you've already used, but use details about life today.

Write Write a letter to a character in the story. Tell them how life has changed and how it has stayed the same. Give examples from each category. For two ways life has changed, tell why you are glad things changed. For another two ways life has changed, tell why you wish things hadn't changed.
    Reread your letter. Does each paragraph have a topic sentence? Do the rest of the sentences begin all the same way? If so, change some so they begin in different ways.

66

Name _____   Date_____

A Wonderful Place

Think & Organize Authors use words to help readers understand how their characters feel about a place. The quote below is from *Charlotte's Web* by E. B. White. The author uses description to tell how the children feel about the fair and what goes on there.

"The children grabbed each other by the hand and danced off in the direction of the merry-go-round, toward the wonderful music and the wonderful adventure and the wonderful excitement, into the wonderful midway where there would be no parents to guard them and guide them, and where they could be happy and free to do as they pleased."

Circle the words and phrases that help you understand how the children are feeling. How do you think the author feels about a fair?

A Wonderful Place

Create a cluster around the word "fair." List what the children might see at a fair, the feelings they might have there, and what events might happen. Reread your cluster and choose one of the events to write a story about.

Pretend you are one of the children at the fair. The next day at school, you tell your friends a story about the adventure you had there.

Create an organizer to show the sequence of events of your story. You might start out with the children being on their own, like in the quote above. Then list the most important things that happen.

Write Use your cluster and organizer for the details of your story. Write the story you'd tell your classmates. Include your thoughts and feelings as well as what happened. Show your excitement by the words you choose.

Reread your story. Be sure your order of events builds excitement. Change it, if necessary. Did you choose words that show your feelings?

Now read what actually happened to the children in *Charlotte's Web*.

Name _____   **Date** _____

The Scene, The Setting, and The Place

Think & Organize Many novels and stories don't give a long, detailed description of their setting. They include details as part of the story. For example, in Walter Dean Myers' book *Scorpions*, Jamal's apartment is not described. In the first two chapters, though, we learn a lot about it.

living room	kitchen	bathroom	Sassy's bedroom
television	stove	bathtub with	
clock on wall	wooden chairs	shower	
couch	radio		
endtable	table		
pullout bed			

Skim a book you have already read and enjoyed. List all the details you can find that describe the setting. If the story takes place in more than one place, choose one to write about.

Title of novel or story:

Setting details:

Organize the details so that all related details are together—perhaps by room or by purpose.

Write Take your reader on a tour of the setting. Describe it, but do not just list words. Instead write interesting sentences to describe it and what is done there. Be sure you stick to the story's setting.

Have a partner visualize the setting while you read your tour to them. Ask them to point out the best parts and the unclear descriptions. Revise and edit your tour.

69

Name _____   **Date** _____

What a Visit!

Think & Organize Think about a story you have read that takes place somewhere you've never been. It might take place on Mars or in the Wild West. List everything you know about that place.

Place:

Details:

Pretend you have just visited that place. Make up a silly, scary, or funny thing that happens to you there. Use the details about the place to create an exciting event. For instance, if you are visiting an Egyptian pyramid, a mummy might invite you to dinner. If you write about a visit under the sea, you could go for a scary ride on a whale's back. Circle the details you will use in your story. List the details of how the event happened. Be sure they are in the right order.

Event:

First,

Second,

Then,

Then,

Finally,

Write Write a story about what happens when you visit this place. Weave your description into the story, rather than describing everything in one paragraph. Remember the same details can tell a funny, exciting, or sad story. It all depends on the mood you create with your words.

Reread what you have written. Do you make the reader feel like they are in the place with you? If not, add more descriptive details. Are the events given in the correct order? Are they easy for the reader to follow? Did you use words that strengthen the mood you want?

70

Name _____   **Date** _____

Full of Fillers

Think & Organize Newspapers and magazines often use small articles to fill space. These articles are called "fillers." Usually they are very short but tell interesting facts about almost any topic.

Choose a book or story you've read recently. Choose a character or event from the book to write a news filler about. Make an organizer with the important or interesting facts about your topic.

Title of book or story:

Write Use your organizer to write a filler of no more than fifteen lines. Think of your audience: people who don't know about the topic. Think of your space: five to fifteen lines. Since you have to interest people who know very little about the topic in a short space, you can't explain much. Use words that create exact images, such as "fleet" instead of "fast."

Have a classmate read your filler. Did you use words that capture the exact idea you want? Could you edit out some words or combine sentences to make it shorter?

When everyone has written a filler, create a newspaper or magazine filled with fillers about the books you've read.

Name _____   Date_____

Like an Eagle in the Sky

Think & Organize

Choose the setting of one of your favorite stories. Create a cluster about that setting. Use words that describe how it looks and feelings that people might have about it. If you choose Scott O'Dell's *Island of the Blue Dolphin*, your cluster might include: shells, canyon, dolphins, the sea, and a harbor.

Title of story:

To develop new images to describe the setting, choose three words from your cluster that can be used to create similes or metaphors. Write the three words and what they will be compared to. Compare them to other things found in the setting's environment. For instance, at the beginning of *Island of the Blue Dolphin*, Scott O'Dell compares an Aleut ship to things found in the island's environment.

"I remember the day the Aleut ship came to our island. At first it seemed like a small shell afloat on the sea. Then it grew larger and was a gull with folded wings."

Write

Write a short description of something in the setting. Use at least three different similes or metaphors in it. Use items from the setting's environment for these comparisons. Be sure they accurately describe the item.

Read your description. Can general words be replaced by stronger, more descriptive words? Did you use complete sentences but not run-on sentences?

72

Name _____   Date_____

Pooh Bear Meets Mary Poppins

Think & Organize Choose a character from a book you've recently read. Write the character's name next to number 1. Under it write the name of the book it is from. Create a cluster with everything you remember about the character. You might write words or phrases that describe how they look, their feelings, the type of person they are or what happened to them.

Choose another character from a different story. Write that character's name next to number 2, write the name of the book or story, and create a cluster about that character.

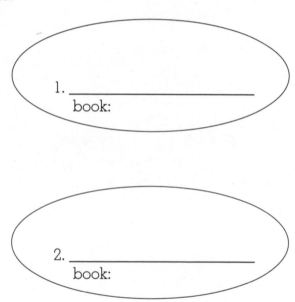

1. _____
   book:

2. _____
   book:

Reread your clusters. Add anything you've forgotten. Create an organizer that shows how the characters are alike and different. You might say they are both boys who like baseball, or they are girls, one of whom likes to read and one who likes to play baseball.

Pooh Bear Meets Mary Poppins

Write Pretend you want to introduce these two characters. Write a letter to one of them. Invite them to your house to meet the other character. In your letter describe how the two characters are alike and different. Tell what they might enjoy doing together. Suggest something the three of you can do together.

Reread your letter. Did you catch the character's interest right away? Did you describe the other character in interesting ways? Is your language correct, but not stiff? Remember, you want the characters to become friends.

Name _____   **Date** _____

And What Do You Think of . . .

Think & Organize   Pick a character from a book you've enjoyed. Create a cluster about that character. Include the kind of person they are, their ideas, what they like and what they look like.

Title of book:

Pretend you are a magazine writer. You are going to interview this character and write an article for a magazine. List ten questions you want to ask the character. Be sure to include questions that will interest your readers. You might also include questions about the events in the story. For example, if you were interviewing Encyclopedia Brown, you might ask him what he really thinks of Bugs Meany or what are his favorite books.

1.

2.

3.

4.

5.

6.

7.

8.

9.

10.

Pretend you are the character, or find someone who has read the same book and ask them to play this role. Answer the questions as if you or the other person were that character.

And What Do You Think of . . .

Write Using the questions and answers, write a magazine interview. Begin with an introduction to the character. Give some important facts about him or her. Then write the interview as if you were with the person asking the questions. You may need to add a few more questions, like "How did you feel then?" to cover all the facts. End your interview by thanking the character.

Reread your interview. Will your introduction catch the reader's interest? Do your questions and answers fit together and lead into one another? Did you use quotation marks correctly?

Name _____   **Date**_____

Poetic Feelings

Think & Organize Choose a character in a story who feels a strong emotion. Create a cluster about how that character reacted when feeling that emotion. For instance, in Beverly Cleary's book, *Ramona the Pest*, Ramona is very excited about going to school. A cluster showing her reactions might include:

Title of story: _____   Name of character: _____

     Add to your cluster ways other people react to the same emotion. Add descriptive words about these feelings and actions.

Write Write a poem about the emotion you've chosen. Include more than one way that people react to it. Use descriptive words and an appropriate rhythm to create your mood. A poem about Ramona might include the lines:

> To school that day Ramona was going,
> But before she left home her impatience was showing.

    Read your poem out loud. Listen to the rhythm and the words you've chosen. Strengthen the pictures and mood your poem creates by using dramatic words and sounds.

77

Name _____   Date_____

Dear Robin Hood

Think & Organize Choose a book or story you have read recently. Pick one character from it whom you liked. List the major events in the story in which the character took part.

Title of book or story:

Character:

Events:

      After each event, write one or two words to tell what you think of it. For instance, after an event from *Robin Hood*, you might write "scary" or "brave."

Write Pretend that the character is your friend. You have just heard about the events in the story. Write a letter to that character. Tell them what you think and feel about some of those events.

      Reread your letter. Did you tell what you thought and felt about the events instead of retelling what happened? Remember the person to whom you are writing already knows what happened. He or she was there! Did you use good grammar and punctuation?

Name _____   **Date**_____

Everybody's Got Problems

Think&Organize Think about a book or story you have read where one character has a problem. It might have been how to do something or how to get along with someone or how to understand someone.

Write one sentence that tells what their problem is.

Title of book or story:

Character:

Problem:

Think about the character's problem. Brainstorm all the ways different people might solve it. List them.

Reread your ideas. Circle the way you would try to solve it.

Write Pretend you are a writer who has an advice column in the newspaper. Write a column about that character's problem. Suggest different ways people can solve it. Then go into detail about how you'd solve it.

Reread your letter. Were you kind? Do your suggestions make sense? Did you use complete sentences?

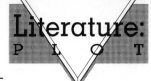

You Are There!

Think & Organize Choose a story in which an exciting event takes place. Answer the following questions about that event:

Title of story: _____

Event: _____

Who took part in the event?

Where did it happen?

When did it happen?

What happened and how did it happen?

Why did it happen?

Pretend you are a radio news reporter covering the event. Plan your report by listing what you will talk about in the order you want to tell it. In your plan include an interview with one of the characters. List a few important questions to ask and what their reply might be. For instance, if you were covering Meg, Calvin and Mr. Murry's interview with IT in Madeleine L'Engle's book *A Wrinkle in Time*, you could interview Calvin. You might ask, "What did you think when you first saw IT?" or "How did you know Mr. Murry could tesser?"

Write Write your news broadcast. Begin with something exciting to catch the listener's attention. Then tell the facts of the event. Include your interview. Make up the answers the character gives to the questions you ask.

Reread your news story. Make sure it is well organized and easy for listeners to follow. Tape record it and listen to it. Edit your report to make things clearer or more interesting.

80

Name _____   Date_____

A Day at a Time

Think & Organize Choose a story you have read recently where a main character solved a problem. Create an organizer to show the choices that character had and when he or she finally solved their problem. For instance, if you chose Janie from Susan Beth Pfeffer's book *Kid Power*, your organizer might begin:

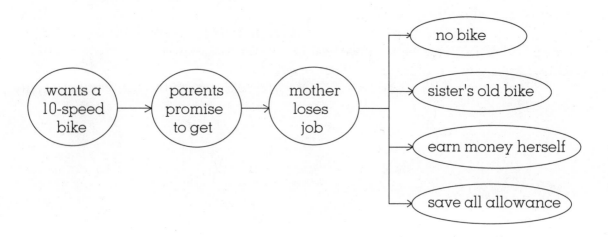

Write Use the information in your organizer as the basis for a diary kept by that character. Write five diary entries as if you were that character. Do the first one from when the character first recognizes the problem and the last one from when the problem is finally solved. The other entries should be from different parts of the story. Tell what your (the character's) thoughts were while trying to solve the problem. Discuss who and what influenced your choices. Be sure your entries are in the correct order.

    Reread your entries. Did you include the character's thoughts and feelings as well as the main events? Did you tell what the character felt when the problem was finally solved. Did you write the entries as if you were writing in a diary?

Name _____   Date_____

Just Because It's Not in Print
Doesn't Mean It Hasn't Happened

Think & Organize In many books, stories, and movies, important events sometimes happen "off-screen." That is, we do not see what happens, but we know that it did happen. For instance, in Patricia's MacLachlan's book *Sarah, Plain and Tall*, we know that Papa picked up Sarah at the train station, but we don't see the event. We have to use our imagination to figure out what happened there.

Choose a book, story, or movie that contains an event that happens "off-screen." Create a cluster for what you know about the event and characters. Add what you think might have happened.

A cluster for the scene between Papa and Sarah at the train station might include:

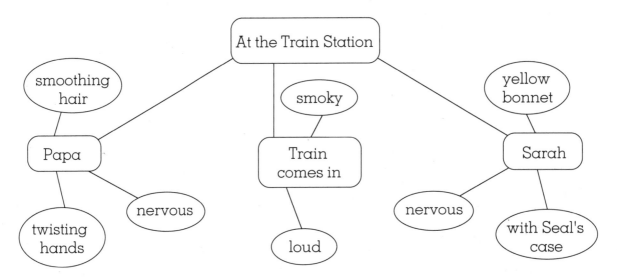

Write Write about this unseen event. Describe the setting, characters, and action. Use details about the characters from the story. Include a prediction about what happens later in the story. Base your prediction on what you know about what happens after this event.

Reread your description. Did you clearly describe the setting and events? Did you use details from the book to make the characters seem like the same ones that are in the book?

82

Name _____   Date_____

Camera, Action

Think&Organize   Pick a book or story you think would make a good TV
show or movie. Pick one scene from the story to make
into a TV script. A scene is one event that happens in one place. If the
actors move to another place, it becomes another scene.

Fill in the information below about that scene.

Title of book or story:

Characters in scene:

Location (where the story takes place and what the setting looks like):

Action (what happens):

The following TV script about Judy Blume's book *Otherwise Known as
Sheila the Great*, shows you a script's form.

*The four girls are outside Mouse's house. It is a big house with two floors
and an attic. It's a grey, cloudy day. Sheila, Mouse, Sondra, and Jane are stand-
ing near a small door on the side of the house. It begins about neck high. All is
quiet, no other kids or adults are around.*

SONDRA: There's a special way to get into the Mouse House when her
mother isn't home.

Mouse turns the handle on the small door.

MOUSE: See, this is where the milkman puts our stuff. My mother never
has to go outside to get it.

JANE: OK, boost me up.

*Mouse makes a step with her hands and Jane goes into the door.
Then Sondra boosts Mouse.*

MOUSE (*from inside the house*): Next!

Sheila boosts Sondra into the doorway.

SONDRA: Help! I'm stuck!

MOUSE: You can't be!

Camera, Action

Write Write your script using the model. First, write a short paragraph to describe the setting. Use the exact dialogue from the book or make up your own. The events in the scene should be the same as those in the book. Don't forget to include sentences that tell the action.

Ask people to read the parts in your script. Have them read the script out loud to you. Do you need to add more dialogue or action so that the scene makes sense? Help someone else read their scene.

84

Name _____   Date_____

From Another Point of View

Think & Organize Choose one scene from a book or story you've recently read. Reread it. Pretend you are in that scene. Close your eyes and visualize what the place looks like and who is there. Create a cluster or organizer describing what you see. For instance, you might choose the scene in Jean Craighead George's book *Julie of the Wolves*, where the hunters' airplane arrives. Your cluster might include:

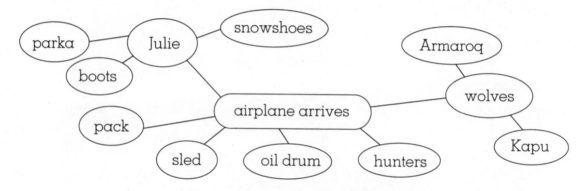

Title of book or story:

List what happens in that scene in the order in which it happens.

Write Choose one object, not a person, who is in the scene. Pretend you are that object. Retell what happens from the point of view of that object. You should describe the same setting and action, but tell what the object sees and thinks. For instance, for the scene with Julie and the hunters, you might take the point of view of the oil drum. It might comment on the warmth it feels when Julie hides next to it or its fear when the bullets are flying.

Reread your scene. Did you use the same setting as in the original story? Did you use a different way of looking at things?

85

From Your Editor

Think&Organize

Think about a fiction or nonfiction book you have read recently. You are an editor who works for a company that is going to publish this book. You have to tell the author what you liked and didn't like about the book. Make two lists: one of things you liked about the book and one of things you didn't like about it.

Title of book:

Liked:

Didn't Like: Changes Suggested:

Your company really wants to publish this book, so you want to make it the best book possible. Reread your "Don't Like" list. For several items on that list, tell how the book could be changed to make it better. You might suggest that the author add more information about a topic or that he or she use a different type of illustration. You might suggest the author describe a character better or give a character a bigger part.

Write

Write a letter to the author. Tell the author what you liked about the book first. Then, suggest changes in a nice way so the author won't get too upset. Remember, you want the author to stay with your company.

Pass the letter to a classmate. Have them read it as if they were the author. Discuss how the author might react and why. Also check your grammar and punctuation. Editors should always use good language skills.

From *The Content Connection*, published by Good Year Books. Copyright ©1991 Hilarie N. Staton.

Name _____   **Date**_____

Words, Words, and More Words

Think & Organize

Select a non-fiction book you've recently read. List ten words from it. These might be hard words, key words about the topic, or unusual words. Do not use names. Write several sentences to define how each one is used in the book. Use a dictionary to help you.

If you chose a book about astronauts, you might list words like: navigator, spacecraft, and orbit. Your definition of navigator would include the jobs of a spacecraft's navigator.

1.

2.

3.

4.

5.

6.

Write

Write a three-part vocabulary test for the six words. Write six multiple-choice questions, two short answer questions, and a writing activity in which students must use some of the vocabulary words.

Try the test yourself. Find someone else who has read the book. Have them take your test. Ask them their feelings about the questions. Edit your test.

Name _____   **Date** _____

Movie Madness

Think & Organize

Choose a movie you really enjoyed. Think about the characters, the story, and how the movie looked. Next to the numbers, list several reasons why you like the movie.

Movie title:

1.
  a.
  b.

2.
  a.
  b.

3.
  a.
  b.

    For each reason give at least two details from the movie to support your opinion. List the details next to the small letters. If you thought the movie was funny, list what happened that was funny. Your details might be: He danced as if he had no bones, or she wore a fruit salad on her head.

Write

Pretend you are a movie critic for a newspaper or a radio or television station. Write a review of this movie. Convince people that it is a wonderful movie and that they should see it. Include your reasons and support each reason with details to make your point.

    Ask someone to be your editor. Have your editor read your review and decide if it is clear and does a good job of supporting your opinion. The editor should also decide if it is too short or too long. Use their suggestions to improve your review.

    Gather everyone's reviews together into a book. Share it so that others can find movies that they might enjoy.

Name _____   **Date** _____

Books Open the World

Think & Organize   Make a list of six books, stories, or articles that you have enjoyed reading. Next to each title tell its subject and whether it was fiction or nonfiction.

Title	Subject	Fiction/Nonfiction
1.		
2.		
3.		
4.		
5.		
6.		

Organize the books into categories. You might have one category with subdivisions for fiction and nonfiction or many different categories. Your organizer might look like the one below:

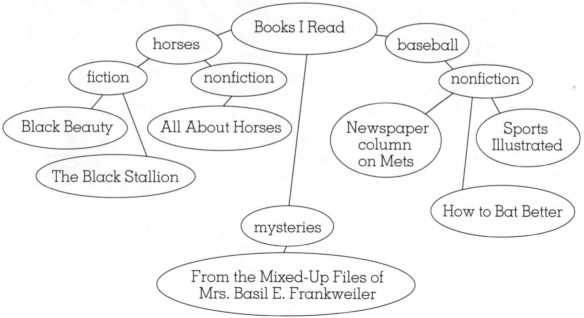

Books Open the World

Answer these questions:

Do you enjoy reading about many topics or just a few?

Why do you like reading about these topics?

What are your favorite books about your favorite topics?

Write Write a speech to give to younger students. Tell them about the type of reading you like to do and why you like these topics. Try to convince them to read about these topics.

Practice your speech by reading it out loud to yourself.

Then read it out loud to a classmate. Be sure you have not used words and ideas that are too hard for younger students to understand. Be sure you have expressed yourself clearly. Support each idea with interesting examples.

90

In science class, one of our main objectives is to teach students new concepts and have them integrate that information into what they already know. To do this, they must use many thinking skills, most of which are also necessary for writing. They compare and contrast types of weather, evaluate the results of an experiment, or apply their knowledge of simple machines to new problems.

In a science learning log, focused free writing activities can help students integrate new knowledge and force them to use specific thinking skills and strategies. The writing itself can help students clarify their thoughts. If they cluster and explain ideas and then list examples, they'll understand the information better and will be better prepared for discussions and complex writing assignments. Give them specific situations and have them apply their new knowledge. For instance, have students cluster in their logs what they know about a specific animal. After they can describe it accurately, have them write another log entry in which they use their knowledge of classification to identify which classification the animal fits, the facts that support that choice, and animals that are related to it. When you read the log entry, you will be able to identify how well they have assimilated the information about classification systems.

Many of the pre-writing techniques described in this book can also be used as independent activities. They can help students organize and understand complex information. Clusters and topic organizers help students determine prior knowledge or evaluate whether or not students have learned a concept. Sequential organizers can clarify the order of an experiment, process, or cycle. Compare and contrast organizers can help students understand classification systems. Cause and effect organizers can help them see the relationship between actions and reactions in both the physical and biological sciences.

Also, these organizers can help students brainstorm, organize, and prepare for writing. As pre-writing activities, they force students to use complex thinking with the science content. They may be required to classify, compare and contrast, interpret, evaluate, imagine, or synthesize the scientific information they are studying. As they work with the data, students understand it better and remember it longer.

Writing should be part of every area of the science curriculum. Students can explain physical science concepts and laws in their own words and give examples. They can write sentences using related words about biology. But students need to do more than just explain science; they need to stretch their thinking and their imaginations using scientific content. They can write a diary from the point of view of a simple machine, a science fiction story about life without a basic law of physics, or a poem about a specific plant, animal, or planet. They can write magazine articles about how a disease affects a family or they can write and illustrate a book of important health rules.

In the thinking and writing activities in this book, students take basic facts a step further than factual lists. In "Dinosaur Zoo" (page 102), they use facts about

a specific dinosaur in a letter to the director of the "Dinosaur Zoo" about the specific living requirements of that animal. Students apply the facts they learn to a new situation.

In "Helping the World's Children" (page 122), they use their basic knowledge of nutrition, health, and safety to write a speech to parents in a foreign country. They must communicate their basic health and scientific knowledge to an unusual audience. In other activities they write television scripts, poems, essays, and monologues. The following list includes other writing forms that allow students to interact with scientific and health information in interesting ways.

By publishing their writing, students develop a sense of pride and of audience. This can take many forms with scientific material. Their reports or "ads" can be displayed around the room and used as teaching tools. They can present or read their interviews, reports, or letters. They can create scientific magazines and books and share them with other students, either in the classroom or through the library. They can share books, speeches, plays, and videos about simple subjects with younger students. They can send letters to real personalities or to scientific institutions. Students (or adults) can take the role of whoever the letter is addressed to and create their own answer to the letter.

In a content subject such as science, students need to think about the data in a variety of ways. In subjects such as health, they need to personalize and humanize the facts. The act of writing can force them to do this while they are using complex thinking skills and pertinent facts. As they do this, their writing and thinking skills improve as does their grasp of the content.

Ideas for Science Writing Assignments

journals or diaries: observations of events (such as weather observations, how a plant grows); of a famous scientific figure; from the point of view of an inanimate object; of a fictional person with a specific health problem

letters: scientist to scientist; to younger or older students to explain a process, or observations; to business people; requests for information; persuasive letters about uses or non-uses of scientific ideas; to important people to ask for change (such as pollution controls)

picture or easy reading books: to introduce scientific concepts (such as simple machines, how plants grow); to present health information; to apply science or health concepts to simple fictional situations

poems: about a topic being studied (such as plants, an animal, stars); to apply or personalize the information learned (such as feelings during a storm, how it feels to be a lever)

Science

stories: science fiction based on: scientific ideas (such as taking a trip through your bloodstream); life in the future; in a different environment; or what would happen if a factor (such as weather) or scientific law (gravity) was changed

fact books: about specific topics

newspapers or magazines
  editorials: about scientific topics and their application

  articles: about new discoveries; uses of scientific ideas; descriptions of scientific ideas; scientific journals; reports of experiments; predictions of the future; travel log of a trip through a process (such as a water drop traveling through the water cycle); fillers about interesting scientific or health facts

  interviews: with scientists; with people who are affected by a concept (such as a desert dweller, someone who lived through a volcanic eruption, someone who had measles); with animals; rocks or machines

  dictionaries: of technical terms necessary for understanding a topic

  technical reports: about a specific process, concept, or item

  advertisements: for new scientific advances; to promote better health or safety

  research reports: of experiments; topic research; scientists; specific problems that need to be solved (such as hunger, pollution)

Name _____   Date_____

Facts of Life

Think&Organize Animals interest people. Nature programs on television often cover cute, dangerous, or endangered animals.
Choose an animal and research its life and habits. Take notes about what you find. Be sure to locate basic information about the animal. Use your notes to create an organizer that includes information about the categories listed below.

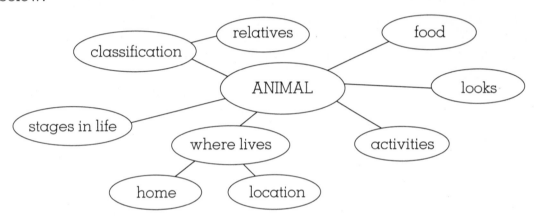

Nature programs for television organize their information and pictures. Number the details on your organizer in the order they will appear on your television show. You may not want to use all of them.

Write Write a script for your program using the format below. The words on the left describe the pictures that will be showing. The sentences on the right are what the narrator will say. An example is done for you.

Picture	Narrator
Close up of a whale	Whales have always fascinated people. They are the largest mammals on earth. Because of their size, they must eat huge amounts of food.

Have a friend read the narrator's part out loud to you. Listen to see if the language is clear, smooth, and interesting. Change anything that doesn't sound right. Make sure all of your facts are correct.

A Scientist's Opinion

Think&Organize Scientists must be very careful to keep the facts separate from their opinions. They use facts to form their opinions, but they don't use opinions instead of facts. Clue words signal a switch from facts to opinions. Read the following paragraph. Underline the sentences that tell facts and circle the sentence which gives the scientist's opinion.

There are only about 50 panthers left in Florida. Most live in the Everglades. They hunt smaller animals and stay away from people. I believe that if we don't do something to save them, in a few years there will be none left.

Pretend you are a scientist and have been asked to nominate the animal of the year. Follow the steps below to help you write a scientific report about the animal you'd like to win that honor.

Which animal will you nominate? _____

Make a list of topics you think should be covered in your report about this animal. Two are suggested for you.

Appearance:

Food:

Research the animal. Take notes about it. Write facts under your topic headings. Add new topics, if necessary. Make a list of facts in your notes that support your idea that this animal should be "Animal of the Year." Be sure your opinions are supported by facts from your notes.

From *The Content Connection*, published by Good Year Books. Copyright © 1991 Hilarie N. Staton.

A Scientist's Opinion

Write Write your report to the nominating committee about your animal. Tell why you think it should be "Animal of the Year." Begin by telling facts about the animal and then your opinion of it. Support each opinion with facts from your notes. Be sure to use signal words to let your reader know when you switch from facts to opinions.

Reread your report. Be sure you have kept opinions out of the factual part of your report. Be sure your opinions are supported by facts. Would your report convince scientists to elect your animal "Animal of the Year"? Have you used good grammar, punctuation, and capitals correctly? You don't want a sloppy letter to spoil your animal's chances!

96

Name _____   Date_____

Baying Like a Foghorn

Poetry is often written about things we're familiar with.
Choose an animal. Create a cluster of everything you
know about it.

In order to create a strong image, poets sometimes use figurative language
like similes and metaphors to describe things. Similes and metaphors compare
two things that are very different. Sometimes similes and metaphors are serious
and sometimes silly, but they always have a true idea behind them. For instance a poet might write:

> Tyrannosaurus Rex is like a castle
> Rising high above the plain.

Go back to your cluster. Circle five things that can be compared to
something very different. Write your choices on the list below.

1.

2.

3.

4.

5.

Next to each item, write how they can be compared (feel, color, size, etc.)
and two to three things they might be compared to. For instance, if you've listed
a bear's fur, you might list "feel" for how they can be compared. Then you might
list "silk," a "kitten," and a "pillow" as comparison ideas.

97

Baying Like a Foghorn

Write Write a poem about the animal. Use similes and metaphors for some of the description. A poem about a polar bear might include:

Like a fluffy pillow,
Soft and white and warm.

Read your poem out loud. Think about the words you've chosen, both what they mean and how they sound with the other words you've used. Change any that aren't quite right. Use a thesaurus to help find new words.

Name _____   **Date** _____

Prairie Shark

Think & Organize

Think about how scientists organize plants and animals. They examine each one carefully to find out how they are alike and how they are different. Use the chart on the next page. In column 1, list ten ways animals can be alike or different. You might include the way they breathe or what they eat.

Pick one animal. List it at the top of column 2 and write down how it does each of those ten things. You might say a shark breathes through its gills.

Then, in column 3, do the same for another, very different, animal. You might choose a prairie dog and say it breathes air through its nose.

Finally, in column 4, create an imaginary animal. It should have some traits of the two animals already listed. Let's say you've listed sharks and prairie dogs. Your imaginary animal might breathe through gills but be covered in fur.

Write

When scientists discover a new animal they study it carefully. They compare and contrast it to animals they already know. They write articles for scientific magazines to share their information with other scientists.

Write a scientific article that describes your imaginary animal. Compare and contrast it to the other animals (show how it is different or alike). Include the facts on your chart. Tell what animal you think it is most closely related to. Be sure to support this opinion with details. Remember scientists want facts to support ideas!

Reread your article. Did you keep to the facts (real or imaginary) about the animal? Is your opinion well supported by these facts? Are your sentences clear and did you use correct grammar?

99

Animal Chart

	Ways Alike Or Different	Animal 1	Animal 2	Imaginary Animal
1.				
2.				
3.				
4.				
5.				
6.				
7.				
8.				
9.				
10.				

Name _____   **Date** _____

Godzilla on Broadway

Think & Organize Read a non-fiction article about an animal. Read another about a place that the animal doesn't normally live. For example, you might read about gorillas and New York City. Take notes about the important facts on each topic.

Animal:

Place:

    Use your imagination to put the two together. List five things that might happen if that animal suddenly appeared in that place. For instance, a gorilla might create a huge traffic jam in New York City.

    1.

    2.

    3.

    4.

    5.

Write Use your list to write a story about what happens when that animal appears in that place. Create interesting and maybe funny events. Use your facts to describe the place, the animal, how it reacts, and how people react.

    Read your story. Does it have a beginning that describes the setting and introduces the characters? Does it have a climax, which is the most exciting part? Does it have an end where the problems are solved? Did you hide your action or make it boring by telling too much information about the animal or the place? Revise your story. Rearrange sentences or events if necessary.

101

Science: ANIMALS

Name _____   Date_____

Dinosaur Zoo

Think & Organize Choose a dinosaur and create an organizer that includes details about the topics listed below. Locate information to complete the organizer.

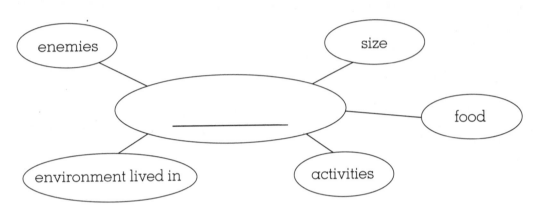

enemies   size   food   environment lived in   activities

Pretend you are giving a dinosaur like the one in your organizer to a dinosaur zoo. You want the zoo to plan for your dinosaur. Reread your organizer. List five things the zoo will have to keep in mind when planning for the dinosaur's space and care. You might list keeping it separate from its enemies or the size of the space it needs.

1.

2.

3.

4.

5.

Write Write a letter to the director of the Dinosaur Zoo. In it describe what kind of space and care your dinosaur needs. Include what the zoo will need to feed it, protect it, and to give it the right environment.

Reread your letter. Are your suggestions based on facts about the dinosaur? Are the sentences in your letter organized so that each paragraph is about one topic? Do all your paragraphs have a topic sentence? Edit your letter.

From *The Content Connection,* published by Good Year Books. Copyright © 1991 Hilarie N. Staton.

Name _____   **Date**_____

The Skeleton Talks

Think&Organize The human body is made up of many systems. Choose one of these systems. You might choose the circulatory system, the digestive system or the nervous system.

List five different things that happen in that system. Some should be normal events, like blood traveling smoothly through the heart. Some should be minor or major problems, like a stomach ache or an ulcer.

1.

2.

3.

4.

5.

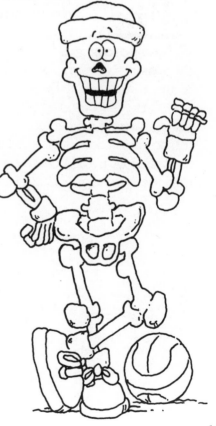

Write Pretend you are that system. Write five journal entries from the point of view of that system. Tell how you work on a normal day and what happens when something goes wrong. Be sure to include what caused the problem and how you (the system) reacted. For instance, the digestive system might complain about what happened the day it was fed lots of junk food at the fair and then had to eat a fancy dinner with lots of creamy sauces.

Reread your journal. Did you stick to problems in your system? Did you use the first person ("I") all the way through, as if YOU were the system? Did you use true facts about the body as the basis for what happened?

103

Name _____   **Date**_____

Like a Rose or a Petunia or a Weed

Think & Organize These words are important to know when you study plants:

pollen   absorption   stamen   seeds   bulbs
roots   germination   photosynthesis respiration   water

Organize the words. Place each one in the category under which it belongs. Add two more words to each category.

Plant Parts   **Plant Needs**   **Plant Activities**

Write Write an essay using the facts on the chart. Write an opening paragraph that describes what your essay is about. Write a paragraph for each category. Use as many of the words as possible. Write a concluding paragraph that restates your main idea.

Have you used each word correctly? Does each paragraph have a topic sentence that introduces your ideas and a concluding sentence or transition sentence that leads into the next topic? Edit your essay.

Purple Mountain's Majesty

Think & Organize Land is constantly changing. Water, wind, and man are often the forces that change it. Choose a place where the land has changed. It might be where a river dug a canyon, where the wind moves sand dunes, or where a deep mine has been dug. Answer the following questions. If you can't answer them, try to find the answers.

What was the land like millions of years ago?

_____

What was the land like hundreds of years ago? Fifty years ago?

_____

What changes happened to the land?

_____

What forces caused these changes?

_____

How did these changes happen?

_____

Did they happen slowly or quickly?

_____

If land had emotions, what feelings might it have had during these changes?

_____

Purple Mountain's Majesty

Write A monologue is a kind of speech that a person tells to an audience. The stories are personal and often they are told in a funny way. A monologue uses the first person (I) point-of-view.

Pretend you are the land. Write a monologue that tells the story of how you've changed over the years. You might include funny or sad stories about what happened there. Tell feelings, as if the land were a person. Don't let your monologue be a dull list of events; make it interesting.

Read your monologue to a friend. Have him or her pick out the best parts of the monologue. Ask them for suggestions to make it more interesting.

Garbage, Smog, and Acid Rain

Think & Organize Pollution has many causes and effects. In each box on the left, write the cause or source of a type of pollution. List the type of pollution in the middle box and the effects it has in the boxes on the right. You can list several causes for one effect or several effects for one cause. Draw arrows to show what causes and effects go together. For instance, car exhaust causes smog, but factory smoke is also a source of smog. Smog causes breathing problems for people. That organizer might look like the boxes below.

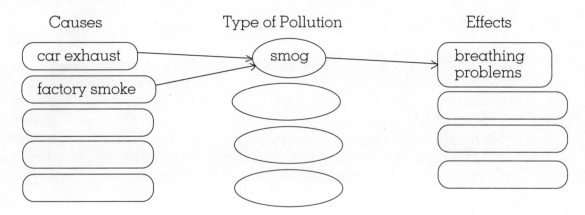

Pick one of your cause and effect diagrams. Redo it with more details. List five details about the cause. For car exhaust, you might list "too many cars" or "leaded gas." List five details about the effects. For breathing problems, you might list "can do less activity" and "lung diseases."

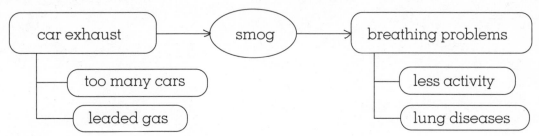

Write Write an editorial that describes the causes and effects of this type of pollution. Try to convince people that it is a serious problem and should be solved quickly. Mention ways people are trying to solve the problems.

Reread your article. Do you use words that make your readers feel something? Remember, they must feel some emotion before they will decide whether or not this is a serious problem.

Name _____   Date_____

Alien Zoo

Think&
Organize Pretend you are a space explorer. You have just landed
on an unexplored planet. The planet is very different
from Earth. Use your imagination and list five ways in which it is different:

Differences:

You find an alien creature there. Since it lives in a place very different from
Earth, it looks and acts different than Earth's plants and animals. Since this is all
in your imagination, you must plan what the creature will look like. Think about
how the creature has adapted to living on that planet. For instance, if the planet
has a very bright sun, it might have sunglasses as part of its face or ears that
shade its eyes. Draw, describe, or create a cluster about what the creature looks
like. Include at least three parts of the alien that fit the conditions on that planet.

_W_rite Write a letter to the Galaxy Zoo. Describe the creature you have
discovered. Tell the scientists at the zoo how the creature has
adapted to its environment and what is unusual about it.
Read your letter to a partner. Have your partner describe or draw the
alien from your description. Decide if you need more details or if is your description is confusing. Edit your letter.

Name _____   Date_____

Starship Captain's Log

 People like explorers and astronauts who "go where no person has gone before" must observe carefully. They draw important conclusions which they pass onto other people.

Pretend you are starship captain. You visit two planets and make entries in your "Captain's Log." In your final report, you must compare these two places and tell what you think about them.

To get ready for this writing activity, prepare a chart like the one below. List facts about two planets. If you are not sure of the facts, look them up. DON'T INVENT THEM. Add more topics to cover the important information about those planets.

Topic	Planet 1: _____	Planet 2: _____
Size		
Location		
Atmosphere		

In order to compare the two places, create an organizer like the one below. The left circle should contain the facts about Planet 1 and the right circle the facts about Planet 2. List the things that are the same for both of them where the two circles overlap.

PLANET 1   SAME   PLANET 2

From *The Content Connection*, published by Good Year Books. Copyright ©1991 Hilarie N. Staton.

Starship Captain's Log

Write Since you are the Starship Captain, you must write the entries in your log. You have just visited these two planets. Write two entries in your Captain's Log. The first should tell about your visit to Planet 1. Tell facts, your feelings, and what you think makes that place special. In your second entry, do the same for Planet 2. Then write your final report which compares the two planets. Draw conclusions and make suggestions about why these planets should be explored, how they can be used by people and what dangers there might be.

Reread your entries. Have you included the important facts and impressions? Have you used words that make it seem like you have really been there?

Science-tionary

 A dictionary lists words alphabetically and tells what each word means. These meanings must be very short and clear. Some words have more than one meaning.

Choose a science topic, like chemistry or rocks. List at least ten terms that are important to understanding that topic. For example, if you choose the human body, you might list: heart, circulation, and brain.

Create a specialized dictionary for your topic. Pick one term and list all you know about it. Read about that term if you need more facts about it. Cross out the facts that are not important or not about your topic. Do this for each term.

Topic:

Terms:

1. _____:

2. _____:

3. _____:

4. _____:

5. _____:

6. _____:

7. _____:

8. _____:

9. _____:

10. _____:

111

Science-tionary

Write After you have researched each term, write one or two sentences to define it. Some words may need more than one definition. Others may only need a few words. For some you might want to include a small picture.

Share your definitions with other students. Find out if your definition is clear enough. They may suggest important information that should be included.

Your final dictionary should list your words in alphabetical order. Each entry should look like a dictionary entry, with the word in darker letters, followed by the definition. Share it with other students when you study that topic.

The Sky Is Like the Ocean

 Choose a science term from this list. Create a cluster for it. Include descriptive words, actions, feelings, or places.

lever   wheel   fossil   rain
magnet   ocean   bone   cell

Choose another science term to compare and contrast to your first term. Choose one from the list or think of one yourself. Create a cluster for it using all the words and phrases you can think of.

These terms may be alike or different in many ways. Look at your two clusters. Answer each questions below by telling if the terms are alike or different and how. For instance, rain and blood are both liquids, but they are made up of different things. Rain comes from clouds, but the body makes blood. Both are at least part water.

Add your own questions to compare and contrast details not covered by these questions:

1. Are they made of the same things or different things?

2. Are they part of the same things or different things?

3. Are they used for the same purpose or for different purposes?

4. Do they come from the same places or are they found in different places?

113

The Sky Is Like the Ocean

Write Write a three-paragraph essay about your topics. Begin the first paragraph with a sentence that states that the two terms are alike. The rest of the paragraph should give details about how they are alike. The second paragraph should state they are different and tell details that support that statement. One of these paragraphs might be much longer than the other. In the final paragraph, draw some conclusions about which is more important, their differences or their similarities.

Reread your report. Do you use specific rather than general words to explain your ideas? Are your sentences clear enough? Do some sentences need to be joined, separated, or enlarged? Revise your essay.

114

Name _____   Date_____

Step-by-Step

Think & Organize   Pretend you are a science teacher for young students. You want to develop a set of science experiments the students can do on their own. Choose a simple experiment, like making a light circuit with batteries and a flashlight bulb. You might choose a weather experiment, an experiment with simple machines, or one with plants. List the necessary materials and each step.

Experiment:

Materials:

Steps:

Write   Write up the experiment. In simple language, tell the students what they will need and what they will be doing. Each step should be in clear and simple sentences that they can understand. Be sure you tell them everything that they need to do in the order they need to do it. Also, give any safety warnings.

Reread your experiment. Did you explain all technical words? Was your language simple and were your sentences short? Is every step listed? Edit your experiment.

Name _____   Date _____

Analyzing a Machine

Think & Organize Inventors and scientists analyze what they've done so that they can improve it. Sometimes they must analyze a complex machine, like the one below.

Complex machines are made up of many "simple machines." If we analyze the first section of the machine below, we find the inventor used two simple machines, a lever to start it and an inclined plane (the rock is pushed up the plane before it drops into the machine). Inventors analyze each part of a machine to see what kind of simple machine it is and how it works. They look closely to see what effect each part has on the action and how other parts affect it. This analysis helps them decide where to make changes. Once they change something, they must then find out what effect that change has on how the machine works.

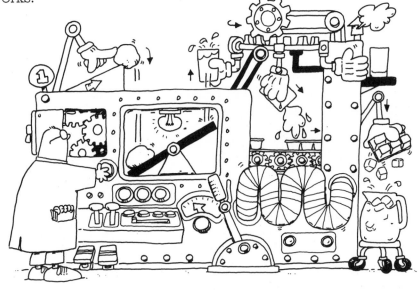

Write Write a scientific report analyzing the parts of a complex machine. Use the machine pictured or invent your own. Describe the kind of work it does. Analyze its parts by telling how the simple machines work together inside the complex machine.

Make recommendations on how to change it into a better machine. Parts of your machine or your suggestions for change can be funny or unusual, but they should fit the situation. For instance you might suggest having a monkey catch the glass of water at the top of machine. However, be sure to keep the tone of the report serious.

Reread your analysis to see that it is clear and descriptive. Will your report convince your reader that you are an expert? Did you use correct grammar? Edit your report.

116

Science: NATURAL PHENOMENA

Name ____________________ Date ____________________

All the News!

Think & Organize Science affects people every day. Weather, volcanoes, and electricity affect their lives. Pick a science topic that affects people. List five ways it can affect them. Don't just list the positive and helpful ways; include problems and disasters it can cause.

1.

2.

3.

4.

5.

Pick one item from your list and write a newspaper article about it. It can be a heartwarming story of how people are helped by it or a disaster story about how people are hurt by it. To plan your story answer these questions.

Who did it happen to?

____

Where did it happen?

____

When did it happen?

____

What happened?

____

How did it happen?

____

Why did it happen?

____

All the News!

Write Write your newspaper story. Give your readers the facts that answer the questions. Tell what you think will happen next.

Reread your article. Did you answer all the questions? Did you use details that will interest your readers and keep them reading? Add a headline to your article. Use just a few words to catch your reader's interest.

Life's a Cycle

Think & Organize Write a report about a scientific sequence of events or a cycle. You might choose the rain cycle, the life cycle of a moth, or the life and death of a volcano.

Research the events. Use at least three sources. One might be a textbook or an encyclopedia. Use at least one nonfiction book or magazine article such as you'd get from the library.

List your sources. Only list the ones from which you get information, not all the books you look at. Include the following information for each source:

Title	Author	Publisher	Copyright Date	Pages Used

1.
Notes:

2.
Notes:

3.
Notes:

Draw a diagram of the sequence. Be sure to show the steps in the correct order. Use arrows to show how the steps fit together. For example, these steps show part of the sequence in a moth's life:

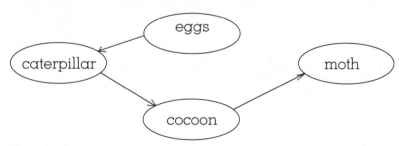

Life's a Cycle

Under each step, list details from your research about that step. For instance, the details about the caterpillar stage of a moth's life might look like this:

> caterpillar
>> eats: leaves
>> lives: on milkweed plants
>> looks like: fat, ugly green worm

Write Write a report about your scientific sequence. Write an opening paragraph that introduces your topic and gets the reader interested. Write at least one paragraph for each step. Use the details from your research to describe the important parts of each step. Write a closing paragraph that makes general statements about the topic. Finally, create an illustration of the sequence. This might be a chart with words or pictures to show the sequence of events or a collage of the steps.

Did you put your paragraphs in the same order in which they happen? Do your paragraphs end with sentences that lead into the next step?

Name _____   Date_____

Ker-Choo, Again

Think & Organize Pretend you are a kindergarten teacher. Many students in your class have colds. You want your students to understand what causes colds and how they can avoid getting them. Create a graphic organizer like the one below. List what causes colds. For each cause show ways the students can try to stay healthy.

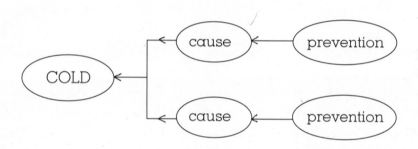

Write Plan a picture book to use with students. It should help them under stand the causes and prevention of colds. It can be a story or a nonfiction book. Write what the text will say on each page and describe a picture to go with the words. The format below is an example of how you can do this.

Description	Story
Page 1	
A small girl with a very red nose is in bed. She looks very sick and unhappy.	Amy has a cold! Have you ever felt like this?

Reread your book. Is it interesting enough for kindergarten students? Do you use too many big words or long sentences? Are the descriptions for pictures complete enough for an artist to understand?

From *The Content Connection*, published by Good Year Books. Copyright ©1991 Hilarie N. Staton.

Name _____   **Date** _____

Helping the World's Children

Think & Organize Pretend you are a children's doctor working in a foreign country where the people have very little money. Many children are sick. List ten things parents can do to keep their children healthy. Use your knowledge of nutrition, safety, cleanliness, and health.

1.

2.

3.

4.

5.

6.

7.

8.

Group items that go together, such as serving healthy food and making sure the child eats. Re-number your list in order of importance, keeping the grouped items together.

Write Write a speech to present to parents in this country. Explain what they can do to help their children. Convince them that they must do these things to keep their children healthy. Remember, though, they are poor and can't afford to buy very much.

Read the speech aloud. Do the words and sentences flow smoothly? If not, try rearranging, substituting, and adding words and phrases to improve how the speech sounds when read aloud.

Name _____   **Date**_____

An Apple a Day

Think&
Organize   Many things, including our health, depend on what we
eat. Keep a nutrition journal for three days. After each
meal, tell what you ate since the last meal. Include the meal you just
finished and any snacks. If you skip a meal, list that fact. Make a statement at
the end of each day that summarizes the nutritional value of what you've eaten
that day.

Day 1
  Breakfast:

  Lunch:

  Dinner:

  Nutritional evaluation:

Day 2
  Breakfast:

  Lunch:

  Dinner:

  Nutritional evaluation:

Day 3
  Breakfast:

  Lunch:

  Dinner:

  Nutritional evaluation:

An Apple a Day

Review the basic food groups. Compare your eating habits with good nutrition by filling in this chart with what you *should* have each day and what you *actually* had.

Group 1 _____

    should have:

    had:

Group 2 _____

    should have:

    had:

Group 3 _____

    should have:

    had:

Group 4 _____

    should have:

    had:

Write Write a report to your parents about your eating habits. Tell where you did well and where you need improvement. Make predictions about how or if this information will change your eating habits and why.

    Reread your evaluation. Did you use the correct terms for the different types of food? Did you use sentences of different lengths? Did you capitalize and punctuate your sentences correctly?

124

Name _____   Date_____

Dear Editor, Safety First

Think & Organize When you form an opinion about something, you think of facts, feelings, and personal experiences.

When a community is deciding whether or not to pass a law about wearing seat belts, people argue about it. Some people are in favor of it and some are against it. Newspapers print articles with the facts. They also print many different opinions. People tell their experiences. Many people write "Letters to the Editor" to voice their opinion. One letter might read:

Dear Editor,
    Most people do not use seat belts, but an accident can happen at any time. You can be seriously hurt, whether or not it's your fault. My uncle was badly hurt when another car hit his. If he had been wearing his seat belt, he would not have been hurt at all. I believe the seat belt law should be passed to save people's lives.
                                        Sincerely,
                                        Edward Hoover

Pretend your community is thinking about passing new school bus safety laws. Pick one law below or write your own. Decide what your opinion is about that law. Cluster facts, personal experiences, and feelings that support your opinion.

Drivers passing school buses with flashing lights will be arrested immediately.

All passengers on school buses must wear seat belts.

Helpers will force students on school buses to sit quietly.

Write Write a letter to the editor of your local newspaper that states your opinion. Use details from your cluster to support your opinion. Try to convince others to believe as you do.

Reread your letter. Have you clearly stated the law and your opinion of it? Have you supported your opinion with clear, honest facts, experiences, and feelings?

From *The Content Connection*, published by Good Year Books. Copyright ©1991 Hilarie N. Staton.

Name _____   Date_____

Crash! Thud! Ow!

Think & Organize Each and every one of us can help make the world a safer place. List five safety problems children can encounter at home. You might list boiling water or falling down stairs.

Problem	Keeping Safe
1.	
2.	
3.	
4.	
5.	

Next to each item, list ways a child can create a safer environment. For instance, you might list "not touching pots on the stove."

Write Write a speech to give to students in the first or second grade. In it you must persuade them that they should take responsibility for their own safety around the house. Give them examples of accidents or safety problems and what they can do to prevent them.

Read your speech to two friends. Have them listen as if they were younger students. Do they understand what you are trying to say? Did you use words or ideas that are too hard for little kids? Do you give convincing arguments? Did you use simple but complete sentences?

126

Social studies is the study of people and their interactions, environment, lives, and history. Creative writing assignments can get students to use the higher-level thinking skills as they analyze, generalize, and personalize the social studies content. By using dry facts in writing, students develop personal feelings, which make history and foreign places come alive to them.

A social studies learning log can help students integrate their new knowledge. They can write from another's point of view (such as George Washington's) or apply facts to new situations (such as what they'll need to cross a desert). Short bursts of focused free writing can help them assimilate facts without having to worry about creating a finished copy.

More formal writing assignments begin with pre-writing, but the pre-writing techniques discussed in this book fit many places as "stand alone" activities. Having students brainstorm or cluster all they know about the American Revolution can give us an idea of their prior knowledge. A graphic overview can introduce specific vocabulary, such as one that lists the geographic regions of their state. A sequential organizer can clarify the sequence of important historical events. Cause and effect organizers can show the causes of historical events, geographical changes, modern global problems, or the results of one person's actions.

Formal writing activities can be developed from some pre-writing assignments. As students manipulate the facts by brainstorming, clustering, and creating organizers, they become more familiar with the facts, see the relationships, remember the information better, and are able to apply this knowledge to new situations. Their thinking skills improve as they compare colonial life to today's life or evaluate the importance of the railroads in settling the west. They might use this information to suggest strategies to a newly settled imaginary country or to debate someone who takes an opposite stand.

In this book, students use social studies information in unusual ways. In "A Marvelous Miracle" (page 135), students write an advertisement for some item that changed life for someone. In "Planning a Vacation?" (page 141), they write a travel article about a specific place. In "Like an Unopened Book" (page 143), they predict and evaluate their own feelings about an upcoming event and write a letter to themselves. In other activities students write letters, editorials, and time travel stories. These types of writing assignments can be done with history, geography, world studies, local studies, and even about their own lives. The following list shows some other writing forms and ways they can be used in the social studies curriculum.

Students can publish their writing about social studies and share it in a variety of ways. Class displays can center around historic people, events, or regions. Students can present biographies to the class to expand their knowledge of an era or event. Class newspapers or magazines can be centered around a specific time or place. Students can publish directions to specific locations or present slide shows to other classes about places they've studied.

Social Studies

Adults or other students can play the role of historic persons, answering students' letters. Letters to real pen pals can expand students' national or world view. Letters to the editor of a local newspaper or in editorials for the school paper can address current issues. Publishing social studies writing can get students involved in many issues and can hook them on the joy of writing.

Ideas for Social Studies Writing Assignments

journals or diaries: fictional ch aracter at a specific place or time (Civil War soldier)

biographies: famous or ordinary people—not only important events in their life, but also how they lived

letters: from a historical character to a modern person or to a person living at the same time; from a modern person to a real or imaginary historical person; to a newspaper editor, present day or in another era; about the importance of a historic event, person, current affair, local issue, or global concern; to a public official

poems: about a place, historic person, or event

radio plays or video scripts: a travel show; a "You are There" presentation; recreate a historic event

stories: of historic events or people; to show life at a specific time

picture or easy reader books: life at a specific time; biography

newspapers or magazines
　　editorials: comment on a historical event from a modern point of view or from the point of view of the time when it happened; comment on current event or local issues

　　articles: report from another time; report a historic event; discuss local issue; travel article about a historic site (in present or past)

fact books: about a person, place, event, or era

directions: guide to the school, neighborhood or an area studied; how to get some place either in the present day or in a specific era; one historic figure sending directions to another

dictionaries: of historic or technical terms; of items used in the past

debates: historic or modern problems and their possible solutions; moral questions

slide shows: about the local area, a foreign place, or historic event

advertisements: travel ad; ad to encourage settlement; ad for a new invention, either present day or in the past

research reports: technical report; geographic features; travel reports; historic events; people

Name _____   Date_____

Home from the Frontier

Think&
Organize   A place changes as weather, people, and buildings
come and go. By putting events in the order in which
they happened, we can better understand the changes.

Bubbling brooks and quiet woods covered the hills. Then the
paper factory was built. Smelly smoke and piles of sludge cover the
hillsides now, but many people have jobs.

If you create an organizer to show how things changed when the factory
was built, it might look like the one below.

bubbling brooks
and
quiet woods   →   factory was built   →   smelly smoke
                                          →   many jobs

Create an organizer that tells about the life of the first settlers in one area.
What was it like when they arrived? What did they do when they got there?
How did they change the area?

Pretend you are one of these first settlers. Think about the facts you've
listed. In your mind, create a picture of life at that time. List what you would be
doing. Also, list your opinions about your life and the place you have settled.
What would you like and not like about life back then?

Write   Pretend you are that settler and write a letter to friends who are
thinking of moving to your area. Tell them the facts and your feelings and opinions about your life as a settler. Tell what the area was like when you arrived
and what it is like after more people have settled there.

Read your letter. Does the information show how the place changed? It
should tell what it was like when you first came, what has been happening, and
how the place is changing. Is that information in the order in which it happened?

Name _____ Date_____

In the Eyes of the Beholder

Think & Organize A writer chooses facts and feelings to help the reader understand a specific point of view. For example, William Pene du Bois' book *The Twenty-one Balloons* uses a first-person point of view. Professor William Waterman Sherman tells the story. The details are those he sees and feels. For instance, when he wakes up on a South Pacific island, we find out what the Professor hears and thinks, not the thoughts of the people who find him.

> I thought that this must be part of some delirious
> dream. The idea of a man who spoke English on a small
> volcanic island in the Pacific seemed so odd.

Pretend it is the late 1800s in the American West. The town of Gruesome Gulch is a small, mountain town. You are there.

Create a graphic organizer of everything that might be seen in the area. Include details of the town and its people. Find out about life in the Wild West if you need more details. Some ideas are listed below.

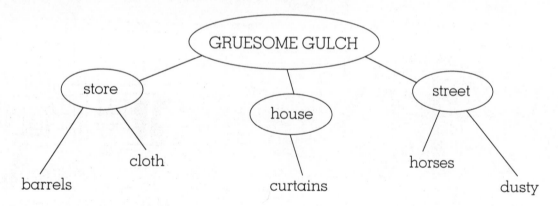

Pretend you have just arrived in the West from an Eastern industrial city. You are used to cities and green farmland. You have never seen a western town before. Put a check mark next to the things on the organizer that interest you. Add other items to your organizer that an Easterner might be interested in.

Pretend you are an Indian who is camped just outside town. You have never been in a "white man's" town before. Put an X next to the things that most interest you. Add other items to your organizer that might interest an Indian.

In the Eyes of the Beholder

Write From the point of view of the Eastern city person, write a diary entry that tells what you notice, what you want to know more about, and what happens to you.

Now take the point of view of the Indian camped near town. Write a diary entry that tells what you notice, what you want to know more about, and what happens to you. Remember the things that interest an Indian are not the same things that interest a settler.

Reread your entries. Did they tell about the same place from different points of view? Did you choose colorful language to describe the place?

Name _____   Date_____

The Not-So-Perfect Past

Think & Organize

Think about what life was like in your area a long time ago. Create a cluster about life at that time. If you are writing about colonial New York, the cluster might look something like the one below.

Dutch language

schools

Hudson River   sloop

COLONIAL NEW YORK   travel

small towns

stone houses   farms

horse   awful roads

Write three problems that people had then. Choose one problem and list five details about it. You might choose travel and list details like "awful roads."

Problems: 1.

2.

3.

Problem:
Details: 1.

2.

3.

4.

5.

Write

Pretend you live in that time period. Write an editorial for a newspaper. Tell about the problem you've examined. Use details to support your opinion of why the problem is important and how it affects people. Predict what might happen if the problem is or is not solved.

Reread your editorial. Be sure your problem and details are about the past. If necessary, rewrite some sentences to make your argument stronger. Have you used complete sentences? Revise and edit your editorial.

If Only You Knew

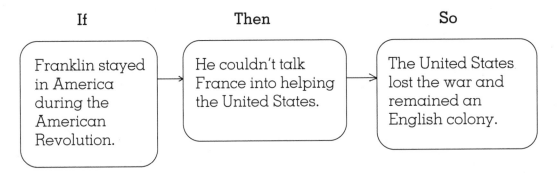

Think & Organize Many famous people took part in the events that shaped our country. Pick one famous American, such as Thomas Jefferson, Abraham Lincoln, Jane Addams, or Martin Luther King. Think about the events in that person's life. Pick one event. Cluster the facts you know about that person, their role in that event, and his or her thoughts about it. Read about the person and the event. Add other facts to your cluster.

Change that person's role in the event. Create an "If . . . then" organizer which shows what would have happened and how history would have been changed if that event had been different. For instance, if you choose Benjamin Franklin and the American Revolution, you might decide that he stays in America instead of going to France. Your organizer might look like this:

If	Then	So
Franklin stayed in America during the American Revolution.	He couldn't talk France into helping the United States.	The United States lost the war and remained an English colony.

Write Write an official letter to a historian. In the letter explain the importance of the person to your historical event. Then, in a few paragraphs, tell how American history would be different if your "If...then" events had happened instead of the real ones.

Reread your letter. Is the change clearly explained and do the events follow a good sequence? Are your punctuation and grammar correct?

A Marvelous Miracle

Think & Organize People never know for sure what will change their way of life. List five items that were important in changing life for people. Tell whose life it changed. For instance, you might list the horse changing the lives of the Plains Indians.

1.

2.

3.

4.

5.

Choose one item from your list. Create an organizer that tells what life was like before and after that item became part of that people's way of life. It might look like the one below:

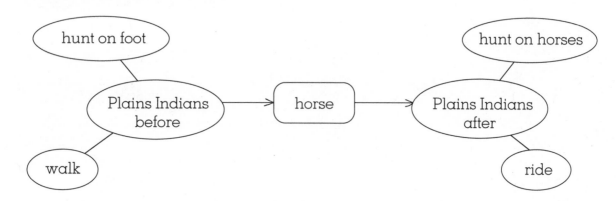

Write Write two different advertisements for the item you've chosen. These can be radio, television, or newspaper ads. Convince people that this item will change their lives for the better. Give examples of how their life might change.

Read or show your ads to a classmate. Ask them if your ads are clear and interesting. Decide if the ads do their job. Do they persuade people to get one of these items? If not, decide what would persuade them and add to or change your advertisement.

135

From *The Content Connection*, published by Good Year Books. Copyright © 1991 Hilarie N. Staton.

Name _____ **Date** _____

Don't Forget the Toothbrushes!

Think & Organize The time is far in the future. You are in charge of ordering goods for a community that is being started on a distant planet. The buildings have already been built. Humans can breathe the air and will be able to grow some food. You must decide what else they will need. These items will be sent on the first spaceships. Make a list of everything you think the first settlers will need for everyday life.

Put these words into several groups or categories. The categories might include foods, business supplies, or furniture. Create as many categories as you need. Add more items. Be sure you have several items for each category.

Write Write a report to the head of the new community. Tell what you are sending. Describe each category and give your reasons for including them. Choose a few individual items and go into more detail about how they can be used. These might include funny things, like trading chocolate bars to aliens, or serious ones, like special medicines for space diseases.

Reread your report. Is your report more than just listing sentences? Do you discuss reasons and suggestions, too? Edit your report so that it shows you know about space and about the needs of people.

136

Corn, Cabins, and Carriages

Think & Organize People have always had the same basic needs, such as food, shelter, and transportation. In different places, these are supplied in different ways.

List three ways people you know get food:

1.

2.

3.

List three different types of shelter people in your area use:

1.

2.

3.

List three different types of transportation people in your area use:

1.

2.

3.

From *The Content Connection*, published by Good Year Books. Copyright ©1991 Hilarie N. Staton.

Corn, Cabins, and Carriages

Research life at a different time. You might choose a tribe of American Indians, a Roman Army, or a castle in the middle ages. Make a list of the ways people got food, their types of shelter, and their types of transportation.

Time and Place:

Food   Shelter   Transportation

Write   Pretend you are a time traveler who is visiting this period. Write a story about how you get food, shelter, and transportation when you arrive. You might meet someone who helps you or you might have to discover these things on your own. Be sure to include how you feel about these new experiences and the mistakes you make. Plan your story with an organizer which shows the story's main events. Then write your story.

Have a classmate read your story. Have them point out the best parts of the story and tell why they like them. Then ask them to suggest places where the story needs to be more interesting. Edit your story with their comments in mind.

138

Name _____   **Date**_____

Armchair Traveler

Think & Organize Many people do not travel far, but do enjoy watching travel shows on television. Choose a place you'd like to visit. It might be a foreign city, like Rome; a national park, like Yellowstone; or an unusual environment, like a rain forest. List all you know about the place and then locate more facts. Make notes of the facts you find. Find maps and pictures that will help your viewer get a better impression of the place.

Place:

Notes:

This travel show has two hosts. One is an adult and the other is a student your age. They are not interested in the same things. Organize your facts into three categories: basic facts that everyone needs to know (for example, where it is); facts that interest adults (for example, population and businesses); facts that interest young people (for example, what to do there).

Basic facts:

Adults:

Young People:

139

Armchair Traveler

Write Use the format below for your television script. On the left, tell what the picture will be. This should be a short description of what you want to be shown. Use the maps and pictures you've located to help you create your descriptions and to list facts for your narrators' speeches. Use maps to tell your viewers where this place is located. In the right column, tell which narrator is speaking and what that person says as the picture is shown. Remember to have your two narrators take turns speaking.

Begin your show with the basic facts. Then give each of the narrators some time to tell the facts that interest them. Sometimes, have them carry on a conversation rather than just tell the viewer about the place.

Picture	Narrators
Distant shot of Leeds Castle	Narrator 1: Leeds Castle is not too far from London, but far enough to be in the countryside.
A closer picture of the lake with the castle in the middle.	Narrator 2: It's built on an island in a small lake, so it seems to have a moat around it.
	Narrator 1: I'll bet it has a damp basement, too.
	Narrator 2: Not as bad as mine, though. They don't build houses like they used to.

After your script is done, choose two people to read the narrators' roles. Have them read the parts out loud while you listen. Show the pictures and maps you've found while the narrators are speaking. Present your show to the class or videotape it.

Name _____   **Date**_____

Planning a Vacation?

Think & Organize Pick a place you have studied. Picture the place in your mind. Brainstorm everything a visitor might see there. Put your ideas into an organizer like the one below. Use the place as the main topic and add details for each category around it.

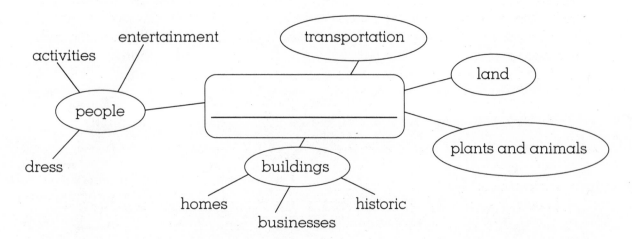

Think about your categories. Think about what a visitor might like to see. If you don't have enough information on your organizer, find more facts and add them.

Write You're a magazine writer. Your assignment is to write a travel article about this place. The magazine will be read by people planning their vacation. Because the visitors don't know much about this place, you have to interest them. You have to give them facts about what they can see and do there. Use only the most interesting facts from your organizer in your article.

Reread your article. Did you begin with something so interesting that your readers will want to find out more about the place? Did you make the place sound exciting? Change words and sentences to make your audience really want to spend their vacation there.

141

Name _____   Date_____

And On Your Left . . .

Think &
Organize   Think about a region of the world. It might be a rain
forest in South America, a grassland in North America,
or a desert in Africa. Close your eyes and visualize what it looks like there.
In your mind, take a walk around the area. Examine the environment: its plants,
animals, weather, and landforms.

Once you have a clear picture in your mind, create clusters about these
topics for your region. If you do not have facts for a topic, locate some and add
them to your cluster.

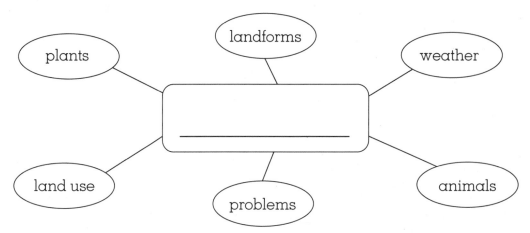

Pretend you are a travel guide in the region. You are taking a group of
people on a tour of the region. Put an X next to the facts in your clusters that you
would include in your talk. Mark what you would point out to them, what you
would be proud of, and problems you would discuss.

Write   Write the speech you would give to the tour group as you travel
through the region. Put brackets [ ] around what you would point to
as you describe it. It might be a plant [barrel cactus] or place [Amazon River].
Tell stories about how people live and about the weather to make it an interesting speech.

Read your speech to a friend. Have them tell you what they liked best and
where you should improve your description. If you are going to give your
speech to a group, find or make some pictures to show what the people would
see outside the windows of their tour bus.

142

Like an Unopened Book

 People's lives are always changing. Each year, your school life changes, too. List details that describe a normal day in your elementary school.

Elementary School:

You probably have heard about what happens at the middle school or junior high school. List what you think happens during a normal day at that school.

Middle School or Junior High School:

Compare the two by placing the details on this chart. If something is the same in elementary and middle school/junior high, place it in the section labeled "Same." If it applies to only one school, place it under the appropriate school.

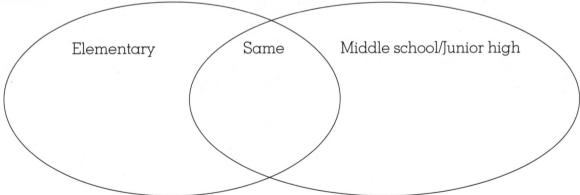

To each side of the chart, write three feelings you have or believe you'll have during a school day at that school.

143

From *The Content Connection*, published by Good Year Books. Copyright ©1991 Hilarie N. Staton.

Like an Unopened Book

Write Write a letter to yourself to be read after you've been in the middle school or junior high for a few months. Discuss your thoughts and feelings about elementary school. Then write your thoughts and feelings about going to the middle school or junior high. Tell about your hopes and fears for the future.

Reread your letter. Did you use comparisons to help explain your thoughts and feelings? Add some interesting ones if you didn't. Did you use paragraphs to separate your main ideas?

From *The Content Connection*, published by Good Year Books. Copyright © 1991 Hilarie N. Staton.